Beautiful Florida

Beautiful
Florida

Concept and Design: Robert D. Shangle
Text: Paul Lewis

First Printing August, 1979
Published by Beautiful America Publishing Company
P.O. Box 608, Beaverton, Oregon 97075
Robert D. Shangle, Publisher

Library of Congress Cataloging in Publication Data
Beautiful Florida
1. Florida—Description and travel. 1. Lewis, Paul M., 1922—
F312.L59   917.59   79-1428
ISBN 0-915796-71-6
ISBN 0-915796-70-8 (paperback)

Copyright © 1979 by Beautiful America Publishing Company
Printed in the United States of America

Lithography by Fremont Litho Inc., Fremont, California

Contents

Introduction 7

The Florida Keys 9

The Everglades 16

Inland Florida 25

Another Country 41

East Side, West Side 57

Enlarged Prints

Most of the photography in this book is available as photographic enlargements. Send self-addressed, stamped envelope for information. For a complete product catalog, send $1.00.
Beautiful America Publishing Company
P.O. Box 608
Beaverton, Oregon 97075

Introduction

How do you set down your impressions of a state that is first one thing, then another? Many commentators on Florida have discovered to their puzzlement that like the squirmy kid in the family group portrait, it won't stand still long enough for a clear picture. Florida is a sometime thing. Sometimes it is a big, flashy, crowded coastal resort dripping with glitter; or it may be a little seaside community where living is simple. Sometimes it's an old town where tradition goes back a long way and the architecture reflects the customs and cultures of a string of different proprietors.

Sometimes it's lakes and prairies, or mangrove swamps and savannahs. It is also concrete and cypress, great rivers and bays, marshes and estuaries. It's lonely islands and crowded ones. It's piney woods, flatlands, and rolling hills, freshwater springs and hardwood forests; it is the New South and the Old South. Florida is rain (55 inches a year) and sunshine (a daily average of more than six hours).

When an outsider hears about the vast numbers of people who live in Florida—about 8 million—and the vast numbers who visit it each year—about 25 million—he may conclude that there is coast-to-coast standing room only. But the state's geological arrangement has meant that large parts of it remain practically empty. Many of its residents, and most of its visitors, are concentrated on the coastal ridges of south and central Florida. In the swamps and jungles of south Florida the alligators may be in the majority. The highland citrus belt has some good-sized towns but to the north and south of it are great pockets of wetlands and hummocks and scrub where people, instead of wildlife, are an afterthought. The canoer and the hiker and maybe the horseback rider can still find such places, some of them as unchanged by civilization as when Ponce de Leon came looking for that elusive fountain in 1513.

P.M.L.

Calla lilies

Whiskey Creek Lagoon, near Ft. Myers

The Florida Keys

You don't have to be from outside of Florida to have trouble naming any of the chain of coral islands, except for Key Largo and Key West, that swing southwestward from the Florida mainland. It's understandable why Largo and West, at the beginning and end, respectively, of the 100-mile arc, are well known. Key Largo got a lot of great publicity from the famous film of the same name made there by Humphrey Bogart and Lauren Bacall. Key West was already famous and prosperous in the 19th century, when Miami and other east coast cities weren't even on the drawing boards. The rest of the keys are only lately emerging from relative obscurity as more and more visitors are drawn down the overseas highway. The blend of sun, deep blue sky, clear shallow waters, and spectacular reef fishing are irresistible.

When the trip to the keys is by land, whatever the vehicle—car, bus, or bicycle—the trip turns into a voyage of discovery. You leave crowded Miami, and signs of human habitation thin out rapidly. After Florida City, US 1 turns from being one of the busiest roads in the world to an uncrowded route through 20 miles of land without buildings or other signs of people. The last mainland segment, before crossing Jewfish Creek bridge to Key Largo, skirts the east side of the southern Everglades, and endless sawgrass "prairies" stretch to the horizon.

Key Largo is the first and biggest pearl in the necklace, with the world's best-known diving area—Jon Pennekamp State Park. Scuba diving and snorkeling are at their best in Pennekamp on the outer reefs a couple of miles into the Atlantic. The world of the reef shimmers with iridescent color. Living coral displays multi-hued, flowerlike formations. Reef fish are all over the shallow water and some of them, like the queen angel fish, show off their own gaudy colors. The more formidable reef dwellers put in an appearance now and then, and for those who may have reservations about sharing swimming space with sharks and barracudas, there are glass bottom boats for viewing the coral.

Part of the interest in a trip along the keys is in the near-miracle of the trip itself. The overseas highway is really a reconstruction of a railway to Key West built by

Florida entrepreneur Henry M. Flagler in the early 1900s and destroyed by a hurricane in 1935. The old railroad bridges still supply the understructure for some of the 42 bridges of the present road. Driving along the Seven Mile Bridge, with the sea on all sides, is a genuine thrill.

The Keys themselves are so varied it's difficult to generalize about them. They range in size from the biggest with whole towns on them, like Key Largo and Vaca Key, to mere pinpoints of coral whose tops are awash in the sea. Many of the bigger keys have sea-related commercial attractions on them, like the coral gardens, aquarium, and Theater of the Sea in the Islamorada group.

The Florida Keys were havens for pirates of the early 18th century, like Sir Henry Morgan and Blackbeard, those villainous cutthroats of the Spanish Main. For many years the keys were graveyards for Spanish galleons and other merchant ships, either wrecked by storms on the uncharted coral reefs or seized by the pirates who left their island coves long enough to appropriate somebody's cargo. Stories still circulate of pirate treasure buried off some of the Keys and of gold and jewels littering the ocean floor off Marathon, spilled by Spanish ships wrecked in a 1715 hurricane. Nobody has found any great treasure, but on Plantation Key there's a sunken treasure museum with some provocative mementos found on the reef by divers, keeping a titillating legend very much alive.

The bigger Keys, such as Largo, are extensive enough to have forests and hammocks of hardwoods like tamarind, mahogany, lignum vitae, and black ironwood. They also grow many kinds of fruit, including the juicy little key limes that have become so celebrated as the chief ingredient of key lime pie, a yellowish concoction that is pure ambrosia. The sea creatures and aquatic birds are not the only wildlife of the keys. On Big Pine Key there is a refuge for the key deer, a very small native species of deer.

Bahia Honda ("Deep Bay") Key, up the road a piece from Big Pine, is interesting from several points of view. It is an especially good area for tarpon fishing. It is also a geological transition point in the keys; from this point to the Dry Tortugas the basic rock is white oölitic limestone and the topsoil is scanty, held together by mangrove clumps and lime trees. Bahia Honda also has one of the few public beaches in the keys. Here, and all along the keys, the changing colors of the seascape bring immense variety to the view. When clouds pass over the sun the iridescent seas turn to indigo; then when the sun comes back, they sparkle in a glittering kaleidoscope of colors, and the nearby keys glow like emeralds.

White Ibis
(Following pages) Pond near Long Pine Key, Everglades National Park

Key West is all "town." On this four-by-two mile coral island live about 30,000 persons. Whether old-timers or new arrivals, they all claim the title of Conch (pronounced "Conk"). The Conchs of the 1800s who made Key West prosperous were a mixture of fisherman, marine salvagers, and merchants—cockneys, Cubans, Bahama natives, and Americans from both the North and the South. The variety of races and backgrounds is still very much in evidence, and the friendly, leisurely way of life is still followed.

The best way for a visitor to see Key West is to walk around it, but most people will prefer to combine some riding (on a tour bus) and some walking. The North and South Roosevelt boulevards combined offer marvelous sea views from the eastern perimeter of the key, but the downtown area and many of the interesting sights are on the western side of the island. Many of the old frame Conch houses, built in the 1800s, are still around. Their unpainted, weathered look gives the island city an extra touch of charm and a feeling of stability. The architecture of the houses is all very individual; most are modest buildings of a story-and-a-half, although some of the more pretentious have two or three floors, with porches extending around three sides.

One of the Key West shrines is the Hemingway Home, now a state museum. The house itself is a white stucco structure, with porches around both of its two floors. Ornate iron grillwork gives it an extra measure of distinction. The property is surrounded by a high wall, enclosing a lush garden where huge banyan trees grow among other tropical vegetation. The house is old (1851) and charming, full of the Spanish antiques that Hemingway furnished it with.

Several blocks north is the Audubon House, where John James Audubon created his paintings of birdlife in the keys. A few blocks east of that is the city cemetery, with its monument to the *U.S.S. Maine.* At the docks on the north the shrimp fleet heaves to. The turtle crawls are here, too, pens that usually contain many captured giant sea turtles awaiting a place on a gourmet's bill of fare.

These are, of course, only a few of the interesting aspects of Key West. It is almost a disservice to the town to call what it has to offer "sights." Very little has been created for the tourist; everything is simply "there," part of the day-to-day life of a resourceful community that has learned to live with and adapt to its natural environment.

Corkscrew Swamp Sanctuary

The Everglades

The Everglades, covering some two-and-one-half million acres of Florida's tip between the coastal ridges, comprise one of the purest wildernesses left in the world. Humankind has made few inroads into this "river of grass," a watery prairie unlike any other kind of terrain on earth. Strictly speaking, of course, there is neither river nor grass in the Everglades. The waters of the Glades are only a few inches to a foot or so deep, spread out over a width of as much as 70 miles. Fed primarily by the overflow from huge Lake Okeechobee to the north, they determine the natural aspect of an immense area enclosed within rocky ridges on the north, east, and west. The so-called "grass" of these watery prairies is really a coarse sedge. It grows very high and has tough, saw-like edges—hence the name "sawgrass."

If a river is a slow-moving body of water, then maybe the Everglades qualifies as a river. The foundation of this enormous swamp and marsh land tilts a bit toward the southwest, so the waters of the Glades flow slowly in that direction. The hard rock of the foundation is oölitic limestone, and is believed to have been the basin of an open sea that covered the area up to about 10,000 years ago. Over thousands of years, sand was borne in by wind and ocean tides, so that gradually the basin filled to a level shallow enough for plant life to exist. Gradually a rich black muck from rotting vegetation has built up, forming a growing medium of immense fertility. In large drained areas of the swamp around Lake Okeechobee, vegetables are grown commercially for the winter grocery demands of the north.

In 1947, Everglades National Park was established, giving protection to 2,120 square miles of subtropical wilderness and to the sometimes rare forms of wildlife which live there. The park takes in the southernmost part of the Everglades and includes environments outside of the Glades themselves. It extends into the waters of Florida Bay and the salt-water estuaries on the Gulf side. Setting aside an area like this involved a long and hard struggle, in spite of its unique and irreplaceable character. The dollar potential of the rich Glades area has had a continuing fascination for developers and has fostered many drainage schemes, even beyond those that are already established to the north around Lake Okeechobee. The future of the

Dogwoods, McClay Gardens State Park

Everglades National Park

Everglades is still not secure; the southern Glades are, of course, dependent for their water supply on the northern portion. Any cutoff of water into the national park areas seriously affect habitat and endanger wildlife there.

One of the rare creatures found in the Everglades is the manatee, a large cowlike aquatic animal of odd aspect and gentle disposition. Other uncommon species with habitats in and around the Everglades are the roseate spoonbill and the great white heron on the Florida Bay keys; and the loggerhead turtle, on Cape Sable. The alligator is very much at home in the Everglades and by its presence assures the survival of other swamp dwellers. Its actively maintained "gator holes" provide water for other creatures during the dry season. The less-common crocodile chooses a salt-water habitat, in the salt marshes and mangrove swamps. In addition to the uncommon bird species already mentioned, some other rarities (in other parts of the country) are regularly seen, such as the bald eagle, the wood stork, and the reddish egret. The park's protective umbrella also shelters endangered plant species, such as the mahogany and royal palm.

There are many ways to visit the park, the extent of a trip depending on one's interests and resources in time and money. The southeastern region can be "done" by car in as little as half a day, by driving the road that winds from the eastern park entrance to Flamingo on the southern tip. Spur roads strike out from the main road at various points, visiting distinctive areas of the swamp where nature trails have been established by the Park Service.

But the park's water-land relationships cannot be deeply experienced until one has taken to the water in a small boat. The Park Service has established a 100-mile route from Everglades City on the Gulf (at the park's northwest corner) to Flamingo. This Wilderness Waterway is for canoeists and proprietors of small boats, and a person has to know what he's about before making this trip. But the rewards are great. The watery trail winds through the mangrove wilderness via creeks, rivers and bays. To negotiate it the boat traveler must be able to read a navigation chart and he must consult with the park rangers at Everglades City before starting out. There are a few wilderness campsites along the way, so that a traveler along this watery highway isn't entirely dependent on raw nature for a place to spend the night during his trip.

A somewhat different version of the Everglades opens up to the auto tourist making the cross-peninsular trip from Miami to Naples or other towns farther up the Gulf coast. Route 41, the Tamiami Trail, is an uncongested, well-maintained two-lane road that cuts through the Glades for 100 miles just north of the national park. The route represents a transportation landmark for the state of Florida. When it was completed in 1928 it linked the east and west coasts of Florida as they had never been linked before, cutting travel time between the coasts from two days to two hours.

(Following pages) Cypress Gardens

The Tamiami Trail goes through the usual sawgrass prairies, but also provides access to other features of the swamp. About 40 miles from Miami, the trail touches the northern border of the national park, where the Shark Valley Loop Road offers views of the park's wildlife. An observation tower is situated at the loop road's farthest penetration into the park. Some of the Seminole villages of the Everglades are lined up along the Trail, offering services to tourists from souvenir shops to airboat rides. The latter activity is an authentic thrill for the first-timer, because the boat sometimes skims over nothing more than damp sawgrass and maneuvers in tight turns around hummocks and other obstructions.

A still more northerly route (State 84) now cuts across the Everglades between Fort Lauderdale and Naples. Completed in 1967, this two-lane toll road penetrates the Big Cypress Swamp. The route doesn't have quite the prestige of the Tamiami Trail and is referred to by long-time Floridians as Alligator Alley.

The northwestern part of the Everglades, not included in the national park and relatively unprotected, has had rough going resisting human incursions. This is the region of the Big Cypress Swamp, serving as an important watershed for the park portion to the south of it. In 1974, some 570,000 acres of Big Cypress were made a national preserve. A piece of the tropics in the subtropics, its climate is mild year round and its terrain, undrained, is a morass. Due to the swamp's constant mild humidity, large numbers of plants found nowhere else outside of the tropics thrive there. Wild orchids and other exotics create vivid contrasts with the cypress foliage. The air-breathing plants that climb the trunks of trees set the swamp ablaze with red, yellow, purple and white for much of the year.

But most of all, Big Cypress is the home of the big cypress. In the Corkscrew Swamp Sanctuary along the northern edge of the swamp grows the largest stand of virgin cypress left in the world. Some of the cypress giants are more than 700 years old and top 120 feet. Corkscrew is 6,000 acres of National Audubon Society preserve, a birdwatchers' paradise: some of its inhabitants are coots, herons, anhingas, grebes, ibis, kingfishers, barred owls, limpkins, pileated woodpeckers, and so on, some rare and some not. Elevated boardwalks take the visitor into the various areas of lake, forest, and swamp.

Among the many good and sufficient reasons for the preservation of Big Cypress as a coherent area is one concerning the continuance of vanishing species. The rare birds whose habitat is the Corkscrew Swamp Sanctuary exist there because conditions are right. The Florida panther, very close to extinction, now is partially dependent on the swamp for its livelihood. Big Cypress is also a winter haven for migratory birds from Central and South America. It is more wild and more remote than the rest of the Everglades, but for all that, not immune from injury inflicted by human intrusion.

Coastal Prairie, Everglades National Park

Inland Florida

It is easy to think of Florida as a long coastline and very little else. But away from the coastal ridges is another Florida quite distinct in appearance and philosophy. The population isn't as thin as it is to the north and south, but in central Florida, small towns are the rule, set among gently rolling hills, and surrounded by the groves of citrus that generate a major share of Florida's agricultural income. The landscape is punctured all over by lakes, especially in the country back of Tampa-St. Petersburg and over to the east side. Citrus is the main concern of central Florida, where the sandy loam is fertile. Farther south, around Lake Okeechobee, cane sugar is grown, as are many other crops. North of Okeechobee is open range land where large herds of beef and dairy cattle graze.

Central Florida has a few big towns, too, but except for the Orlando area, not much on the scale of the coastal watering places. Lakeland is the next biggest community, and still of quite manageable size—around 42,000. Its name derives from the presence of 11 lakes within the city limits. Lakeland and the pleasant small communities that cluster around it have a pleasing sense of permanence and established tradition.

The Florida Citrus Commission, which controls crop quality, has its headquarters in the town. A good third of Florida's citrus is produced in the region around Lakeland. Other foodstuffs are grown here on a large scale, like winter vegetables and strawberries, but the citrus groves are central Florida's trademark. This is the highland region of Florida, one of the few large inland areas fertile enough and dry enough for growing oranges, lemons, and grapefruit.

There are so many lakes, most of the region seems to be under water. (Of Florida's 58,000 square miles, 4,000 *are* covered by water). A good way to gain some comprehension of it all (and enjoy a scenic treat on a grand scale) is to take a low-altitude flight over it in a small plane. Citrus groves, jungles, swamps, and lakes of many sizes and shapes make up a multi-textured landscape. Some of the lakes are merely algae-filled scars in the earth created by phosphate dredging operations. (Bartow, 14 miles southeast of Lakeland, is the center of a phosphate industry that

Cypress, Highlands Hammock State Park

produces one-third of the world's supply and $100 million annually for Florida's economy). But the "dead" lakes are comparatively few, and the main impression is of a beautiful watery paradise on which the marks of civilization are quite moderate. Even the sprawling freeway from Tampa to Orlando loses its bluster among the natural charms of the countryside. And Walt Disney's Magic Kingdom, up near Orlando, seems strangely toy-like from the air, even though it is a very large spread.

There are plenty of tourist attractions in central and north-central Florida, and for the most part they are a pleasing blend of man's art and nature's. The towns themselves, like those around Lakeland, seem to be appropriate parts of the landscape, because their scale doesn't overpower it. Auburndale and Winter Haven are these kinds of places, and they have the additional distinction of being close to Cypress Gardens, one of the most esthetically (and commercially) successful parcels of managed nature that human enterprise has produced in Florida. Cypress Gardens is a formerly obscure swampland and lake that has been prodded and promoted into 164 acres of natural beauty. The widely promoted water-ski shows on Lake Eloise are great crowd pleasers. But for those who stay and look around the Gardens, there may be more enduring pleasure in the enjoyment of the lavish plantings of tropical and subtropical flora from many parts of the world. Stone walks take visitors past artfully designed and precisely executed beds of azaleas, roses, camellias, and gardenias. The Gardens are a highly romanticized version of the Old South, but there is nothing wrong with that. In the midst of beautiful lawns are crimson bougainvillea, many varieties of palm trees, heavy philadendron vines, poinsettias, and so on. Huge cypress hung with moss rise out of the lake, and winding waterways offer boat passengers intimate glimpses of exotic plant and even animal life. The Gardens are, in sum, a remarkable combination of human planning and skill, and a benign Florida nature's ability to produce extravagant growth.

A few miles to the south is Lake Wales and its Mountain Lake Sanctuary. The Sanctuary's centerpiece is the celebrated Bok Tower, standing on Iron Mountain (the highest point in Florida at 324 feet above sea level). This is another example of art and nature in a tasteful, spectacular combination. The Sanctuary, with its magnificent grounds and gardens, is a salve for the soul, and a refuge for many kinds of birdlife. The 205-foot gothic tower and its carillon are a graceful memorial to Edward Bok. The tower's facing is coquina rock and pink and gray marble. Surrounded by a moat, and projecting dignity as well as beauty, it enhances the mood of serenity that extends through the sanctuary. There are bamboo "blinds" looking out on a feeding area where visitors may observe and photograph the birdlife. An extra touch of beauty in the tower moat is provided by brilliantly colored wood ducks:

Florida Homestead Bayfront Park
(Following pages) Sunset near Winterhaven

Japanese Park and Garden, Miami Beach

rufous breast, black-and-white-striped head, iridescent green and violet crest and back of head, and the body, a lustrous combination of green, violet, blue, and black.

Rural interior Florida and its endless groves of citrus reach north from the Lakeland region into Clermont and beyond. A relaxed drive along uncrowded US 27 is a good way to see this scenic countryside—rolling hills and valleys laced with streams and little lakes. Closer to the Gulf side, another road (US 19 from Tampa) accomplishes much the same thing for the coastal back country. This route gives access to two of Florida's 27 marvelous big clear water springs—Weeki Wachee and Homosassa.

North beyond the main citrus belt is what used to be Florida's scrub country. It's a swamp and hummock landscape whose wildlife and people of the past were so vividly evoked in Marjorie Kinnan Rawlings' *The Yearling*. Today the people still live off the land, but the emphasis has shifted somewhat. Ocala now rules over a horsey establishment that has largely replaced a strictly agricultural one. Horses have been popular here for some time, but not until its thoroughbreds began to win some of the big races did it begin to take on a reputation to rival Kentucky's blue grass country. Florida's ranches thrive on ideal conditions—plenty of good, grassy pastureland on rolling hills, limestone-filtered water of great purity, and fine weather.

One of the sources of that sparkling water is near Ocala. Silver Springs is the all-inclusive name of some 150 natural springs that flow into a common basin at a combined rate of about 800 million gallons a day. Tours of the springs may be taken in glass-bottom boats that penetrate the 65-foot-long cavern where the main spring is located. The boats also visit the various pools, observing plant life formations 80 feet or more down, plainly visible through the perfectly clear water. Mastodon and manatee fossil remains have been found there, indicating that these creatures once lived in the warm (72 degree) springs. The 100,000-year-old springs are fed by Florida's abundant rainfall, which passes rapidly through the sandy surface layer and is absorbed into the thick underlying limestone. The water of this immense reservoir then gushes to the surface wherever there is a handy opening in the earth.

Florida's big Ocala National Forest is just next door to Silver Springs. The Ocala is typical of the area's rolling forest and lake country, and many kinds of outdoor activities are possible within the forest's 362,00 acres. It has its own springs, too, with white sand beaches. Winding through the lush forests are streams on which visitors can drift in canoes provided by the Forest Service.

North from Ocala to Gainesville is a segment of Florida that still has a lot of Old South charm. The towns in this 35-mile stretch are quite attractive. The old houses, spreading oaks, and the springtime-flowering dogwoods and azaleas all help fill in a picture of the traditional Southland. Gainesville itself has antebellum mansions which these days may be helping to house students of the big and bustling University of Florida.

Fifty-five miles southwest of Gainesville, just off the Gulf Coast, are the Cedar Keys. Cedar Key, the town, is on the largest and nearest island. The tiny outer islands are a national wildlife refuge. The remarkable thing about Cedar Key is that the town was once on its way to big-time development and never made it. Now it is a quaint and quiet fishing village on a white-sand island connected by a causeway to the mainland three miles away. In its boomtown phase, it was a railroad terminal and steamship access point to South Florida. It was also a lumber town, making cedar slabs for pencil factories in the North. When the nearby mainland cedar forests got too far away, the railroad eventually went by it to Tampa. Then Cedar Key settled back to become what it is today, a quiet place on a beautiful and lonely part of the Gulf Coast. It is likely to remain out of the way and unnoticed for a long time. No through highways are anywhere near it—US 19 is 23 miles inland at this point. And it has no railroad any more. Cedar Key seems pleasantly anachronistic in a state where many such communities never seem to stop growing. The town provides a glimpse into a quieter time in Florida's history, and demonstrates the variety available in Florida to travelers willing to go a little out of their way.

Dogwood, Torreya State Park

Palmetto and Slash Pine, Ochlockonee River State Park
(Following pages) Cape Florida Lighthouse, Key Biscayne

Tiger Lilies, Cypress Gardens

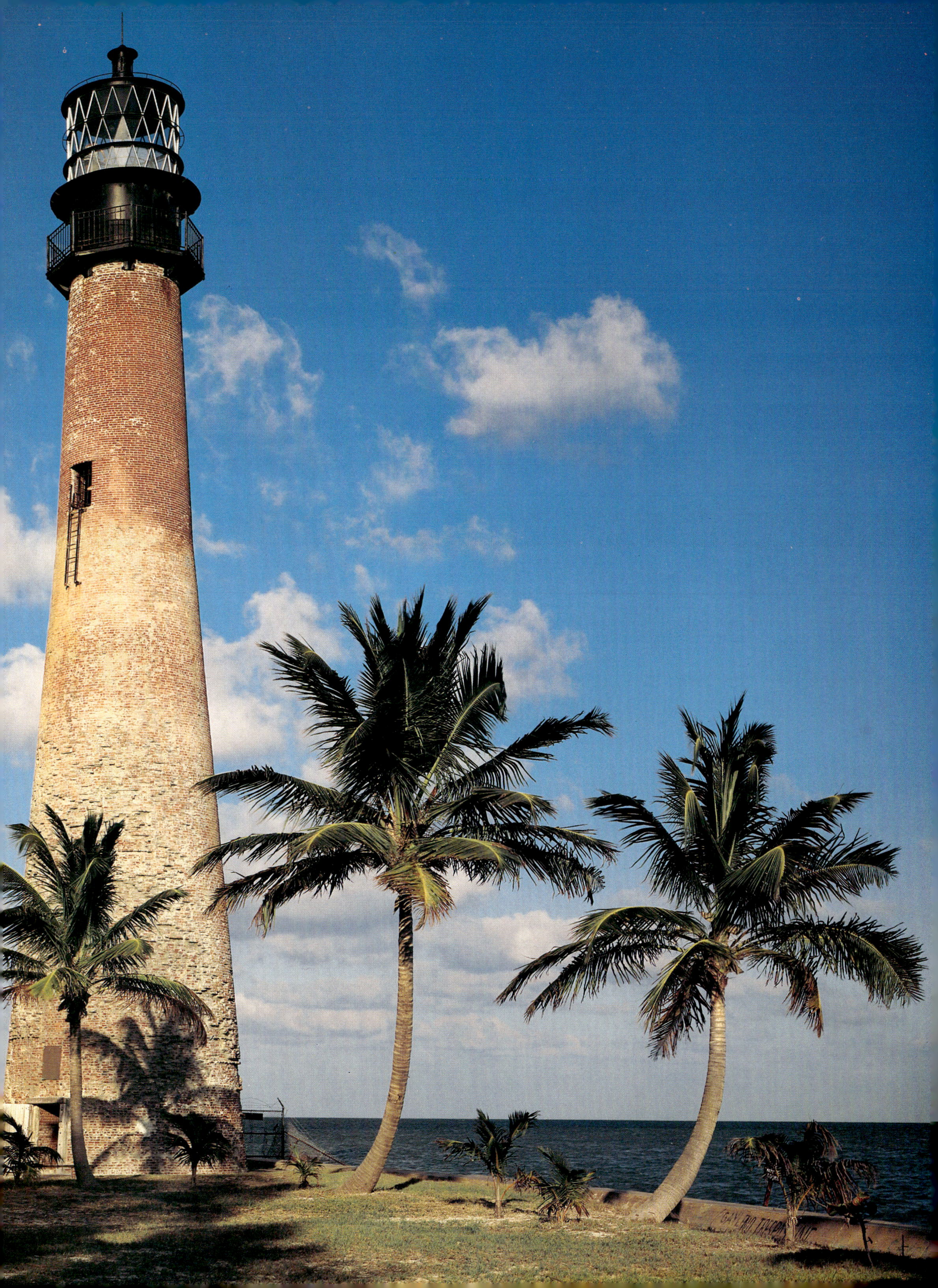

Eola Park, Orlando

Gulf Islands National Seashore

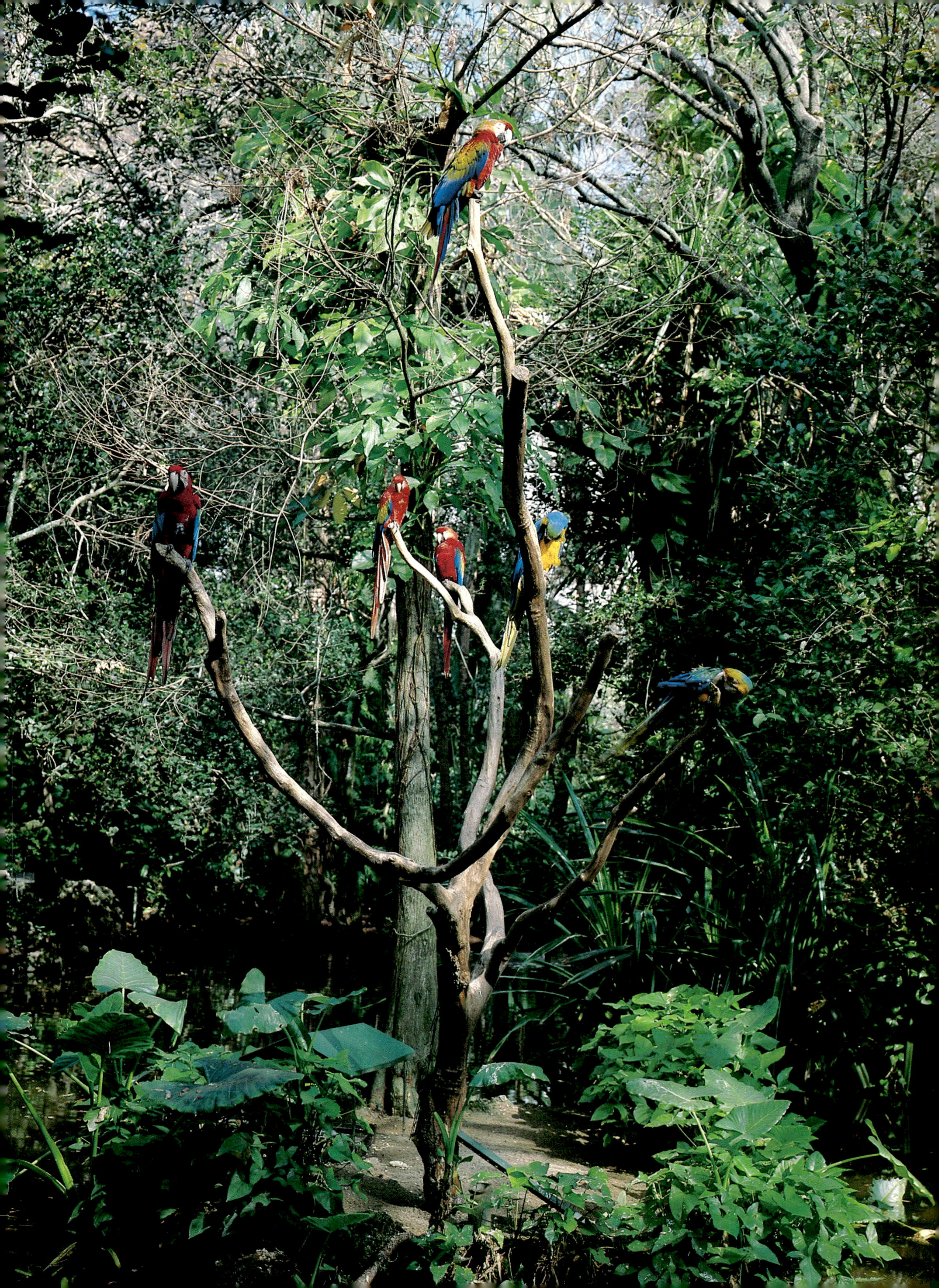

Another Country

The Suwanne River glides out of the Okefenokee Swamp on the Georgia-Florida border and wanders lazily through northern Florida, turning this way and that on its journey to the Gulf of Mexico a little north of Cedar Key. The river is an approximate dividing line between a heavily promoted tourist Florida and a land of piney woods, swamps, small farms, and fishing towns that has changed very little since John Muir walked across the wilderness of north Florida a hundred years ago. To oversimplify a bit, there is the peninsula and there is the panhandle.

The panhandle country is comparatively empty land. The pine forests of the flatlands are interrupted occasionally by fields of sugar cane, cotton, and tobacco. The liveoaks, with their graceful drapery of Spanish moss, grow where the soil is more fertile. Around Tallahassee and westward, the terrain begins to look more like that of Georgia: the contour becomes hilly and the soil is red clay.

In the vast emptiness of the pinewood flatlands and hummocks—little knolls where hardwood trees grow—the people seem to merge with the forests. The region has only three far-flung cities: Tallahassee, Panama City, and Pensacola. All are separated from each other and from the rest of Florida by miles and miles of flatwoods, swamps and hummocks—countryside where solitude is easy to find. People live here, but they are not the kinds of people who band together in big communities. The independent spirit of the folks in this region is well known. There is a surprising degree of national and ethnic diversity: Western Europeans, Spanish Americans, Scandinavians, and Eastern Europeans all seem to share the sense of belonging to the land.

You might think that Tallahassee, being the capital of Florida, would have its own tourist atmosphere, like the state's other major cities. But the only long-running show in town occurs just a few months out of the year, when the legislature meets. When the lawmakers and the lobbyists depart, Tallahassee is quiet. It's a very pleasant town, and quite isolated, ringed by swamps, wildlife sanctuaries, and the Apalachicola National Forest. It is 200 miles from Pensacola on the west and 168 from Jacksonville to the east, with very few populated places in between.

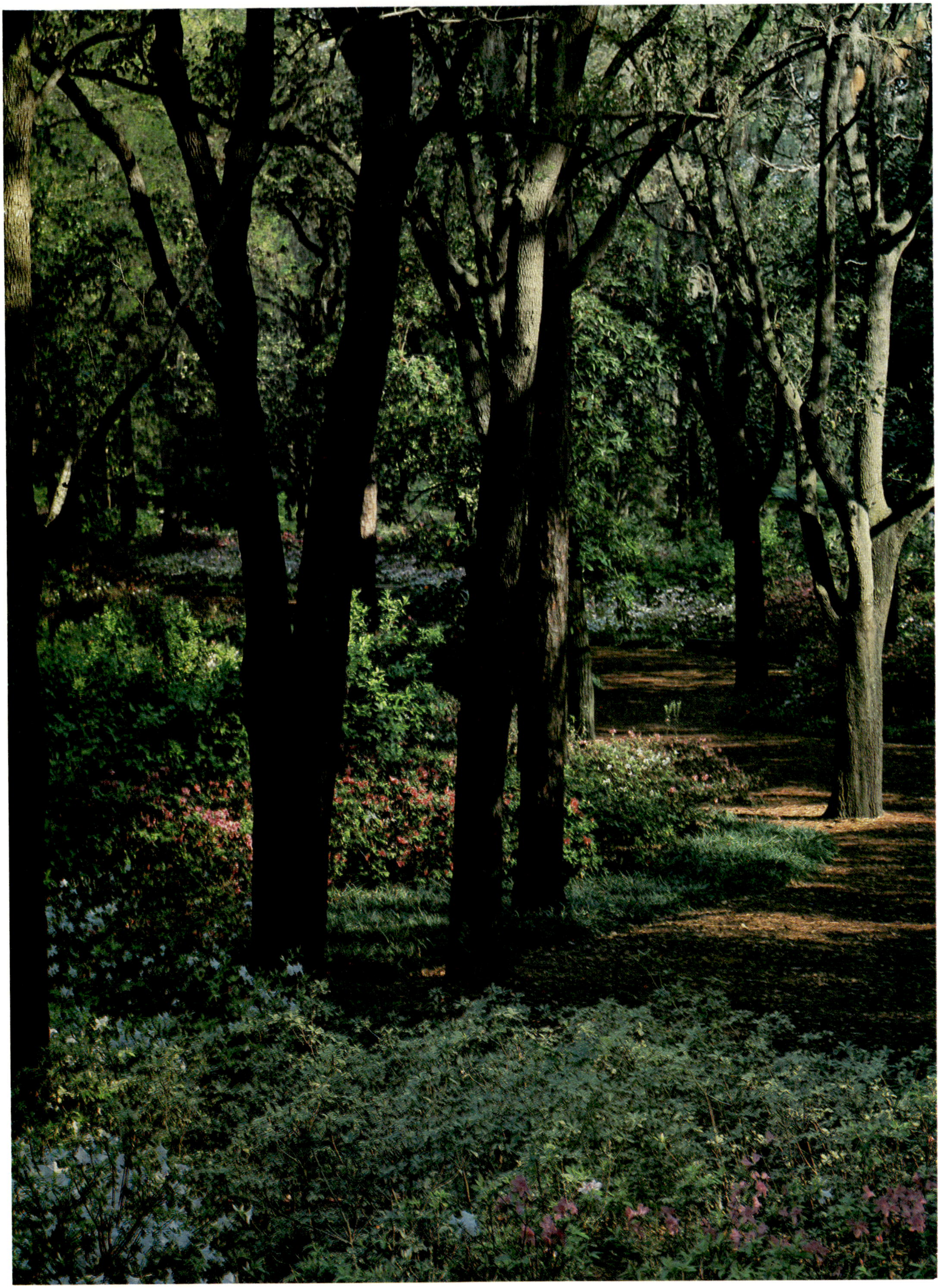

Woodland garden, Singing Tower and Mountain Lake Sanctuary

Sunrise at Florida Bay
(Following pages) Flamingo Lake, Parrot Jungle

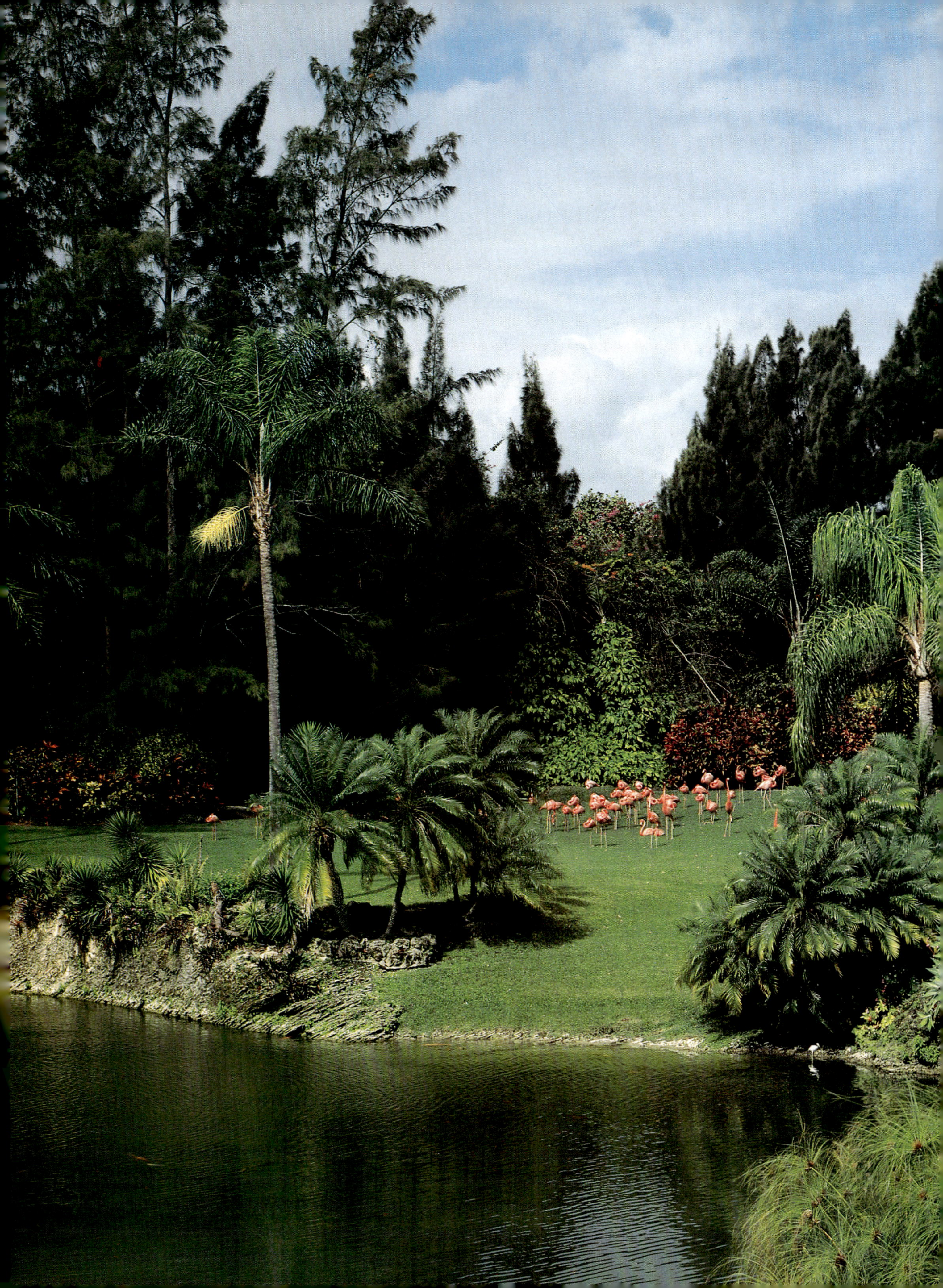

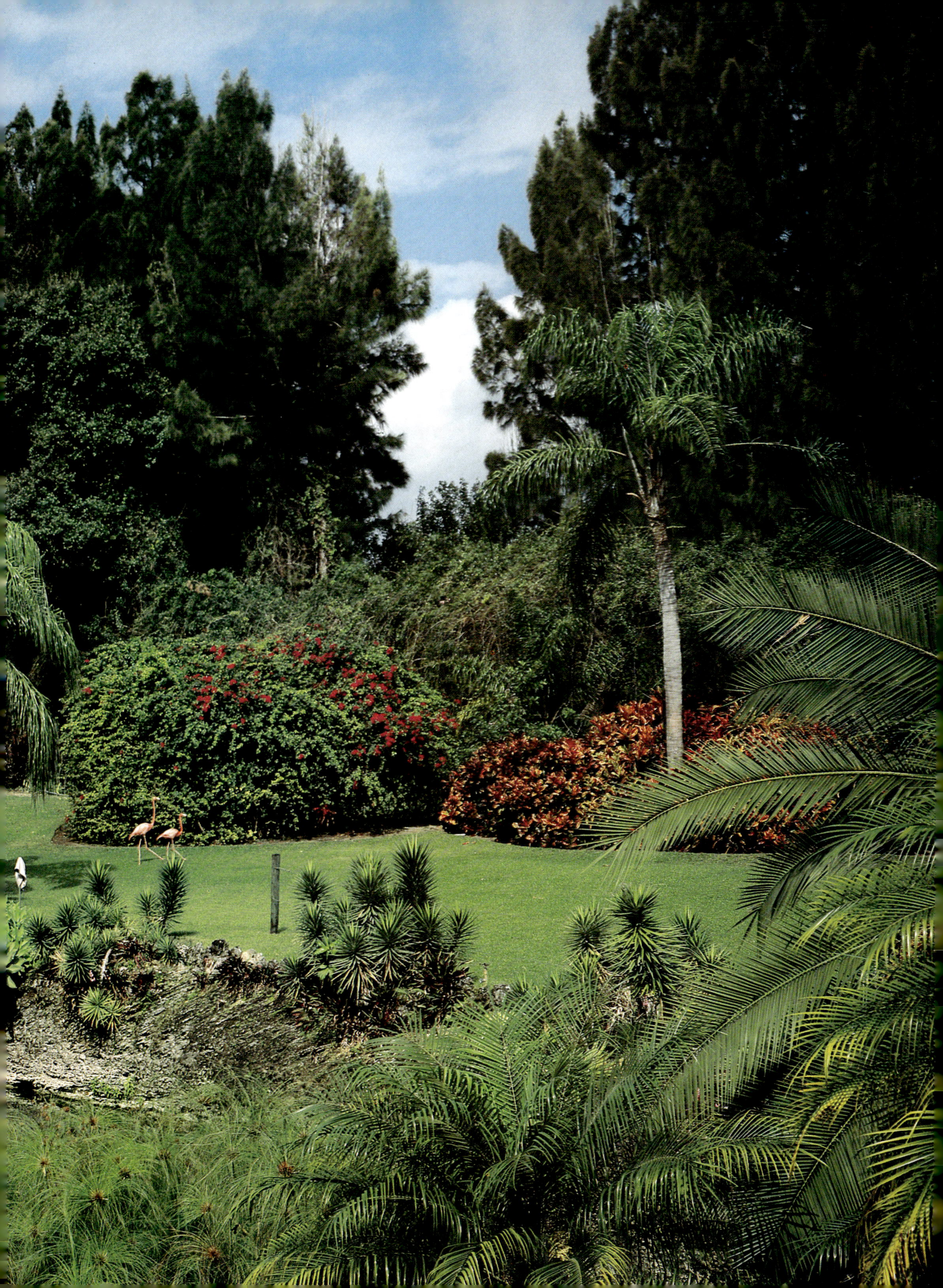

Lake Cherokee, Orlando

Singing Tower, Mountain Lake Sanctuary

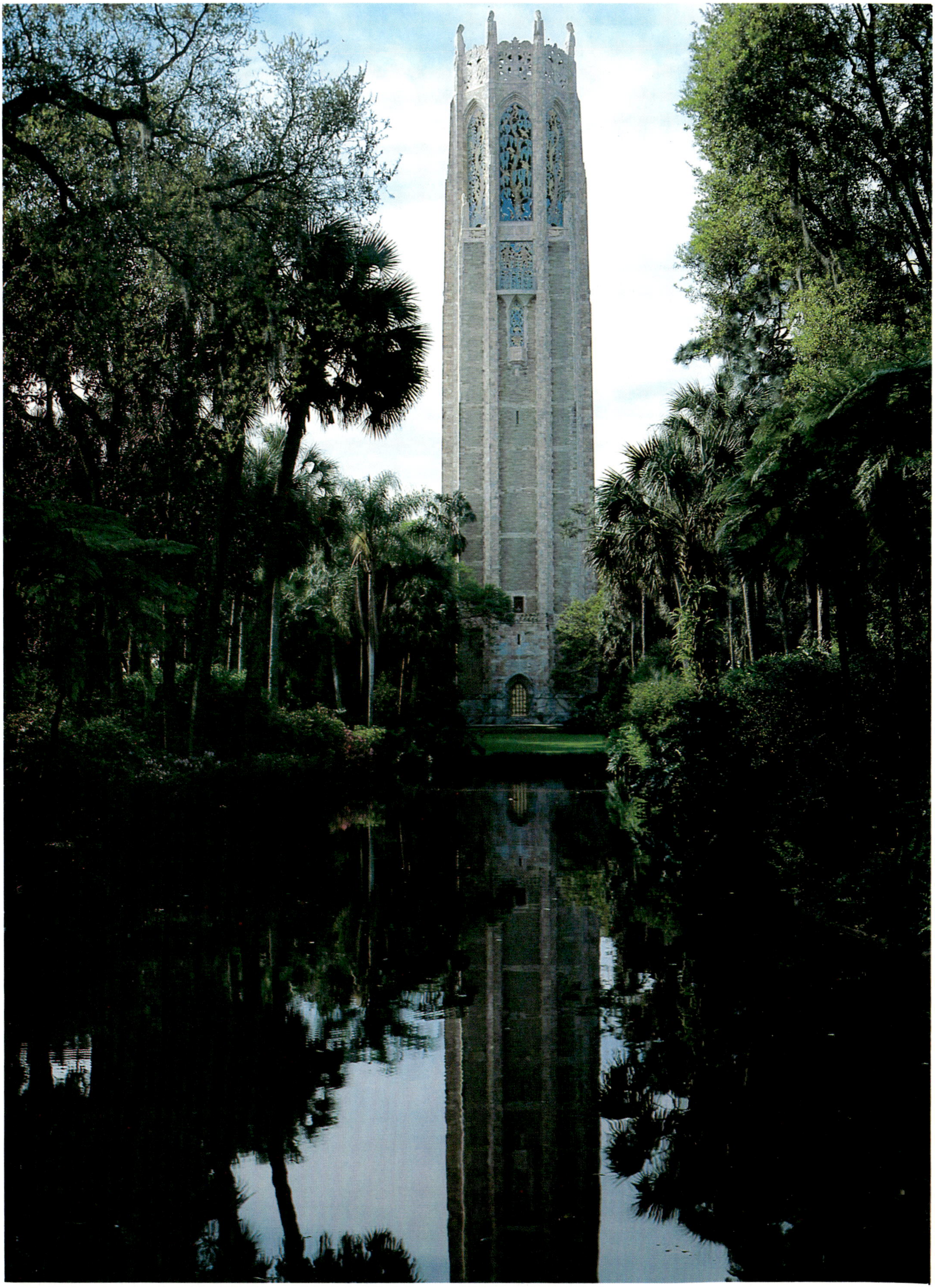

The capital city is no sleepy backwoods village in this period of rapid growth for Florida. Tallahassee's population is around 75,000 and its range of activities includes much in addition to government. Florida State University is a large presence, along with Florida A&M. But the town is still basically Old South, in looks and in societal strata. It is built on the hills that make the terrain of north and west Florida so different from the rest of the state. It has antebellum mansions and beautiful old liveoaks that spread their giant branches over wide streets. All over town there are floral displays, their fragrance and beauty epitomized in lavish gardens of honeysuckle, camellias, and azaleas. The blend of pine woods and swamp outside of town brings its own ingredient to the aromatic mixture. One of the most glorious concentrations of flowers, in this state of flowers, is just a few miles north of town. In the springtime the 308 acres of flowers and blooming trees at Maclay Gardens State Park are at their peak.

The Gulf Coast beaches of the panhandle extend 100 miles from Apalachicola to Pensacola and are called with shy modesty by area chambers of commerce "the Miracle Strip." And they do represent a kind of miracle in Florida, where beach access by the public is so often closed off by beach front developments. This curving shoreline has more public beach than all of south Florida combined. Because it's cooler country than the south, it is where the summer beach visitors go. The natural attractions of the blue, translucent Gulf waters, the pine-rimmed bayous, the stark-white, quartz sand beaches, and the cool, fragrant air make these beaches among the state's loveliest. Most of the visitors these days are families from Georgia and Alabama, coming for sunbathing, swimming, fishing, sailing, and water-skiing.

Pensacola, at the western end of the Gulf beaches, is a very old city with a very rough reputation. It's checkered career began with an ill-fated Spanish colony in 1559 that succumbed after two years to violent Gulf storms and unfriendly Creek Indians. Pensacola didn't actually become a city with a continuous history until 139 years after this, in 1698, when a second attempt at a settlement was successful. Even though it loses out on this technicality as the "oldest city," Pensacola once a year celebrates its founding as such, thereby ruffling the promotional sensibilities of St. Augustine, the officially recognized oldest city, on Florida's northeast coast. St. Augustine was founded in 1565.

Oldest or not, Pensacola has been, and still is, a very colorful town. Even after it finally made it in 1698, the town didn't enjoy the luxury of stability as to nationality or place of residence. Five different nations have claimed it at one or more times, amounting to 17 changes of ownership. And the town has been moved from the mainland to Santa Rose Island (a narrow offshore strip) and back again.

Royal poinciana, Ft. Myers

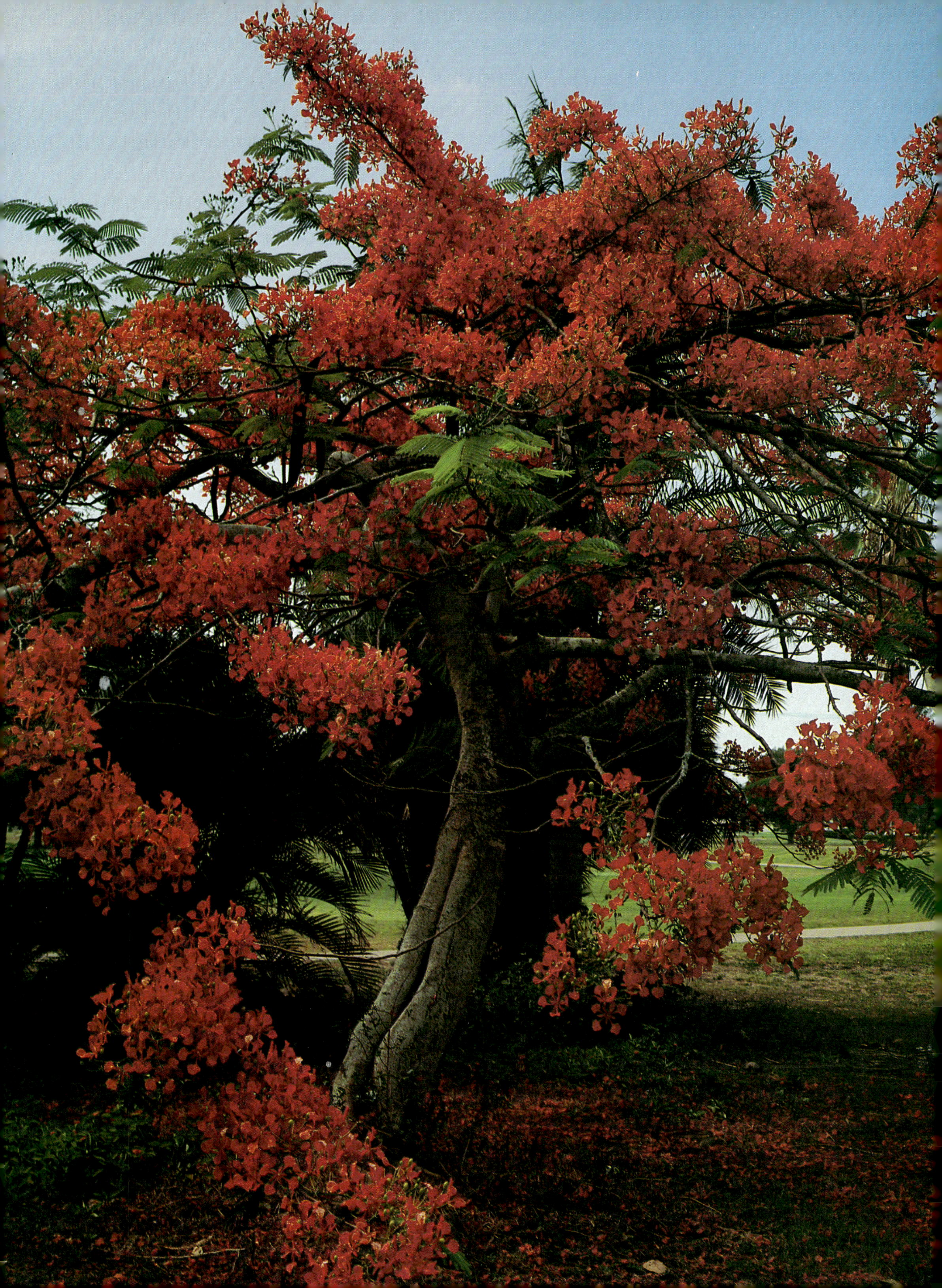

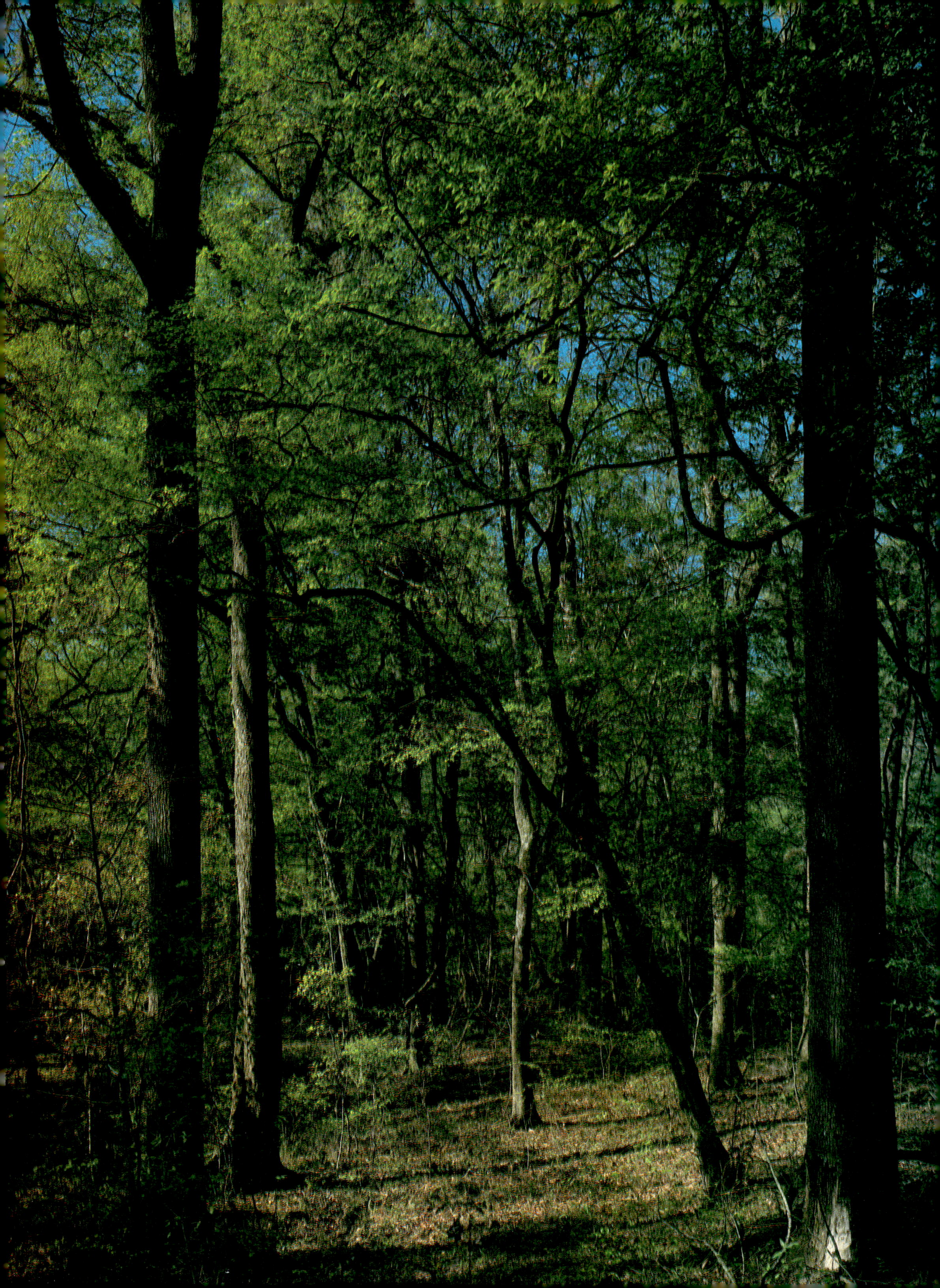

Some of the brutal episodes in the town's history began occurring after the Spanish, moved by Pensacola's prosperity under British colonists-traders, recaptured the town in 1781. In a few years all of the British had left and the vacuum was filled by renegades, cutthroats, drunks, and assorted adventurers who gave the town a bad reputation. Andrew Jackson slipped down over the border in 1818 and brought some Jacksonian law and order to Pensacola while evicting a combined British-Spanish-Indian defense force. But perhaps the most unsavory chapters in Pensacola's history were written after the United States gained control. Jackson himself, in brief tenure as governor, failed to accomplish much in reforming the town.

After Jackson's departure gambling houses were reestablished along with the tradition of waterfront brawling. The fights and the frolics lasted up to the Civil War, when the Confederate Army left the city to the Feds, who were encamped in Fort Pickens and so controlled the entrance to Pensacola Bay. Pensacola stopped growing during the war. And when the vast pine forests were finally logged off, the lumber export trade disappeared and the mills closed down.

What Pensacola lost in timber and export business during the last of the 19th century, it made up for in the early years of the 20th. The first World War brought another boom. The decision in the twenties to make Pensacola the country's naval air capital gave a new security and stability to the town's economy.

Today's Pensacola may not be as rough and tough as during parts of its hectic past, but its Spanish background still flavors the life of the city. The appearance of the old part of town is reminiscent of Mobile and New Orleans. There are lofty balconies and intricate wrought-iron railings, balustrades, colonnades, and gables. Much of the natural growth of the area—oak, magnolia, and other hardwoods—remain, bringing mellow beauty to the residential streets and park areas on the hills overlooking the old town. In the names of its streets, such as Intendencia, Gonzales, Moreno, Palafox, and Zarragossa, part of the Spanish heritage is also preserved. More of it survives in monuments commemorating Spanish victories over the French and in the olive skin and dark eyes of many Pensacolans descended from those early Spanish pioneers.

This admixture of cultures and races in an impressive physical setting of bay, bayous, and ochre bluffs makes for a living and colorful town. Pensacola has always been that, and will be, very probably, for a long while. It has the promise of the new university (West Florida) and a new industry (tourism) to bolster the contributions of the Naval Air Station. It could very well become one of the scarce places in the world where man and nature have combined to put together a truly superlative habitat.

Although Pensacola finally ran out of forests near enough to provide a livelihood, the panhandle has plenty of pine woods left. All along north Florida, on

(Following pages) Bahia Honda State Park

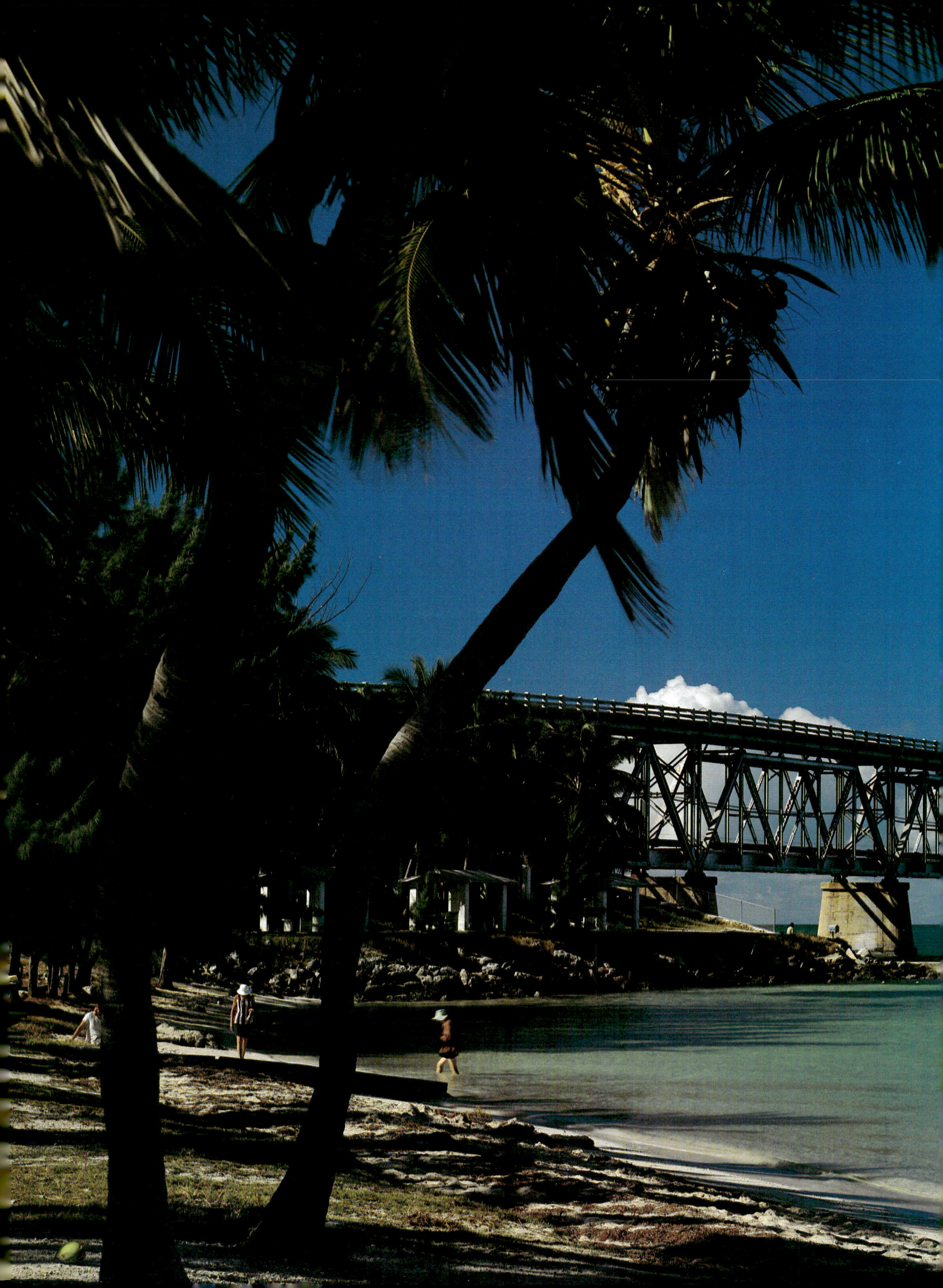

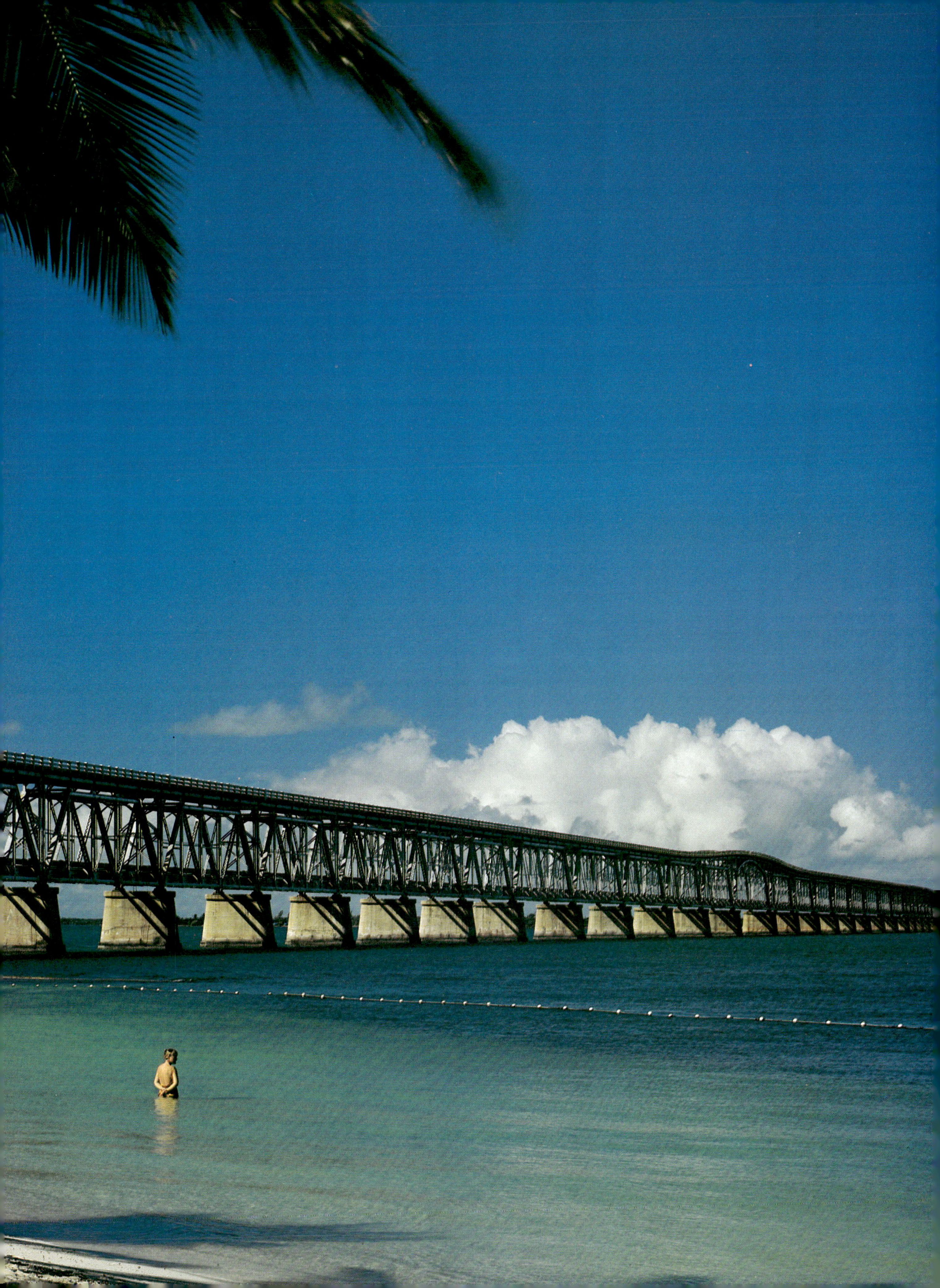

the coastal plain and back up into the hills, the pine forests roll on endlessly. In the dry flatwoods, turkey oaks grow up between the wide-spaced pines; in swampy areas palmettos cover the open spaces.

The Apalachicola River, cutting through the fat part of the panhandle, is the setting for some of Florida's biggest trees. Some virgin forests are still left here. The valley of the Apalachicola is an astonishing blend of apparently anomalous plant growth, with hot-weather and cool-weather varieties standing in neighborly proximity. This occurs at Torreya State Park, which occupies a hilly site along the river not far from the Georgia border. Here is the rare Torreya tree, which grows only in the Apalachicola River valley. The park contains other rare specimens, like the Florida yew, along with southern pines and northern hardwoods.

The middle of north Florida (between the Apalachicola and the Suwannee rivers) is characterized partly by cotton and tobacco plantations, especially in the northern counties, and partly by wilderness. Cypress swamps dominate, and hummocks of oak, bay, cabbage palm, and magnolias are laced with Spanish moss and long, looping vines that bar passage to all but the most determined forest wanderers. Some of these ambulatory species may be human, others may be a variety of Florida fauna, chiefly alligators, panthers, bears, deer, and rattlesnakes.

A little river that could truthfully be called the epitome of wild Florida is the Wacissa, a bit southeast of Tallahassee. It's one of those slow, southern streams that invites the solitary dreamer, either on its always-green banks or canoeing lazily along its hyacinth-choked waters. The Wacissa glides purposefully, yet peacefully, through dense forest with scarcely a ripple disturbing its placid demeanor.

Slash Pines, Everglades National Park

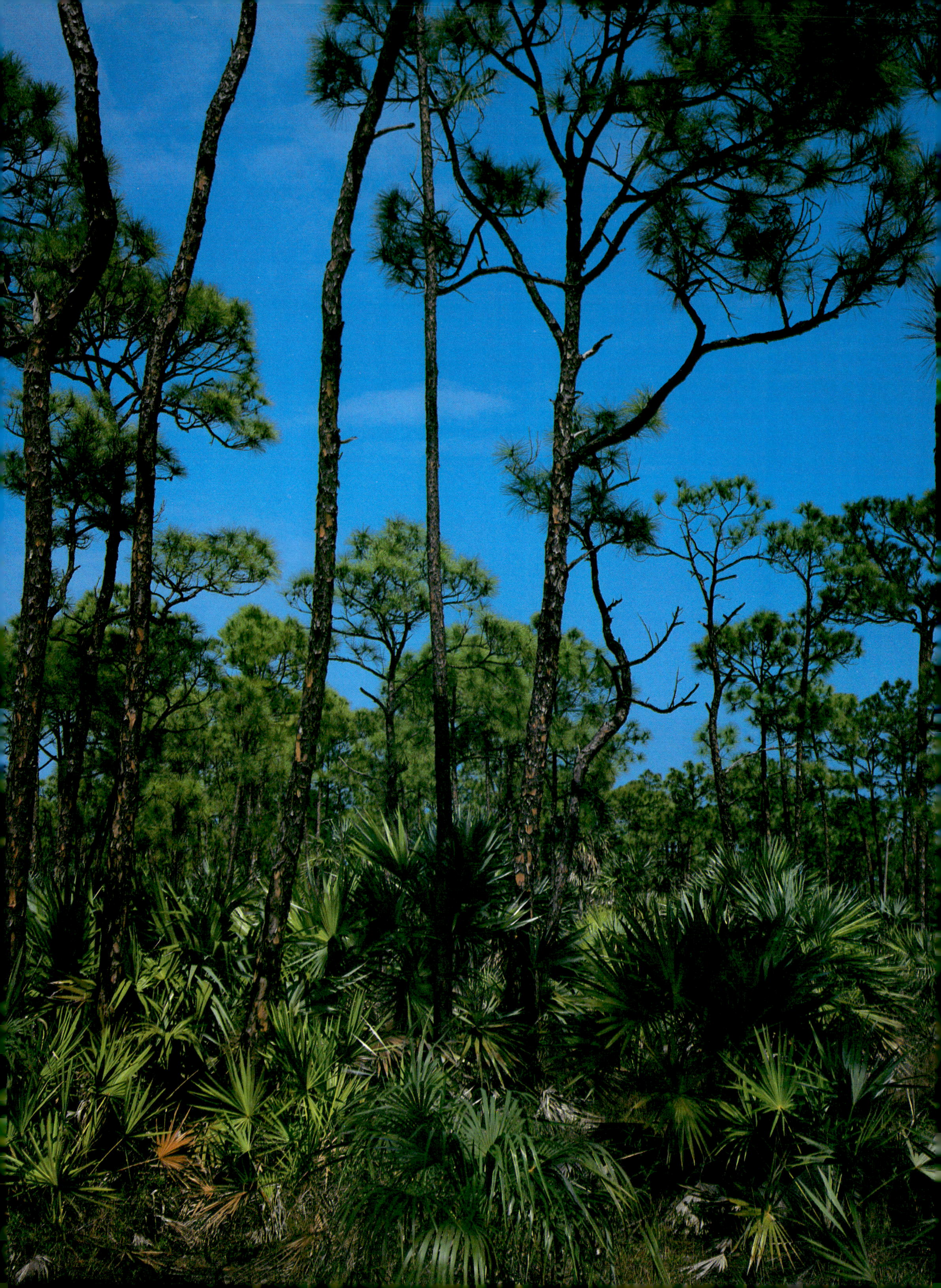

East Side, West Side

The profile of the Florida peninsula reminds some cynics of a cocked pistol, ready to relieve the tourist of his cash. The truth is that coastal Florida, with more miles of shoreline than any other state except Alaska, attracts tourists—and cash—in a much gentler way. The gravitational pull of Florida's winter sun is so powerful that it nearly depopulates certain communities up north during the season of ice and snow. The famous white-sand beaches on both Atlantic and Gulf coasts enrich the recipe. Indeed, the physical endowments of Florida are so obvious and overwhelming it seems redundant to talk about them.

Tourist development by itself is reason enough for many people to go somewhere, and Florida has many examples of lavish resortery along its coasts. If the visitor investigates the many possibilities, he can find something quite to his taste and budget among coastal communities, within that much ballyhooed realm of subtropical sun, glorious weather, and beautiful, clear seas. When a person goes somewhere, he makes a choice, and there are all manner of choices in Florida.

One of the choices is St. Augustine, the oldest city on the continent, 40 miles north of Daytona Beach. The feel of mellow antiquity is a genuine attribute of this cultural treasurehouse. Symbols of old Spain are the predominant motif—St. Augustine is a Spanish city before all else, having been founded as a Spanish settlement by Don Pedro Menendez de Aviles in 1565. The British and finally the Americans took possession when the Spanish were ousted once, returned, then left again voluntarily in 1821, when Florida was transferred to the United States.

The Spanish influence shows in much of the architecture, ranging from the 16th century to the 20th. The very earliest building is the mission of Nombre de Dios, founded on the same day as St. Augustine. Close by the mission on Matanzas Bay is the Castillo de San Marcos, near the old city gates. The Castillo is pretty "new," in St. Augustine's time scale. It was not completed until 1756, with the help of Indians, slaves, soldiers, and city residents. The enormously thick walls (12 feet at the base) of the Castillo are surrounded by a moat. The huge, four-sided structure was designated a national monument in 1924. During the period of the Seminole Wars,

Key Deer Refuge, Big Pine Key

Suwannee River State Park

Fern Garden, Highlands Hammock State Park

the fort served as a prison for some of the important Seminole leaders like Osceola and Coacoochee.

Structures of varying ages are scattered over the compact downtown area, fronting on streets like narrow, cobbled St. George Street. Some are opposite the Castillo and along with the old fortress served as part of the city's defense system. The gates were built in 1804, of coquina rock, replacing others erected in the previous century. Across from the city gates, on St. George Street, is a small building of handhewn cedar planks called the "oldest schoolhouse," but built as a residence in 1778.

Farther south along St. George Street is the Old Spanish Treasury, a two-story stucco house that was a private residence for most of the 19th century. The original building is believed to date from around 1600. On Charlotte Street, a block east of St. George, is a two-block collection of old homes and shops called San Agustin Antiguo in which the arts and crafts of the Spanish and English colonists are practiced by skilled artisans wearing the costume of the period.

On the south side of town are more buildings of varying antiquity. The two-story "oldest house," dating from the late 1500s, is partly original, partly restored, with low ceilings supported by great beams, massive fireplaces, and floors of crushed coquina rock. The St. Francis Inn, nearby, has had a varied career from the time the Franciscans first erected a church, monastery, and convent on the site around 1577. When the British controlled the town they housed their troops at the Franciscan church. Later on, when Florida became a United States territory, the monks' cells became jail cells. And during the War Between the States, it was a spy headquarters.

St. Augustine is several kinds of old, and some of its atmosphere of bygone days comes from a more recent period. The ghost of Henry M. Flagler is pretty active in some parts of town. The indefatigable Mr. Flagler, Florida's supertycoon of oil, railroads, and hotels, came to town in the 1880s and began the city's development as a winter resort. He extended his Florida East Coast Railway south from here and built two huge and ornate hotels. The railroad and the hotels are still operating, although the hotels have given up their original function.

The Alcazar Hotel was built in 1888, modeled after the Alcazar of Toledo, Spain. The building now houses the city hall and the Lightner Museum with its vast collections. The immense and lavishly ornamented (inside and out) Ponce de Leon Hotel occupies six acres of landscaped grounds nearby. Its exterior features a red tile roof, many minarets, domes, and spires, and intricate arched gateways. The Ponce de Leon is now Flagler College. Inside there are 300 rooms of luxurious dimensions and opulent appointments—just the thing for college students who want to study in style.

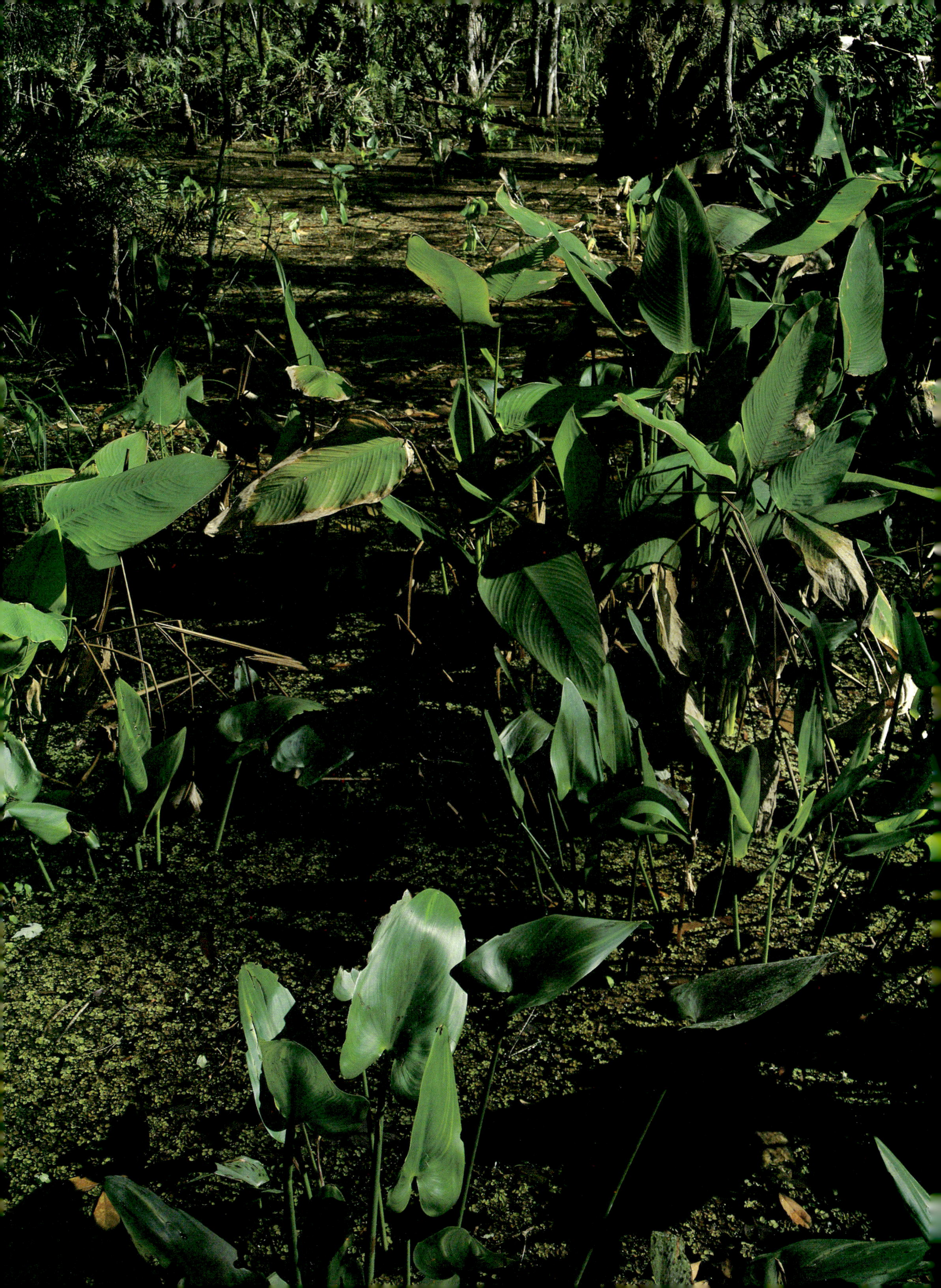

Ft. Castillo, St. Augustine

Alligators, Alligator-Anhinga Trail

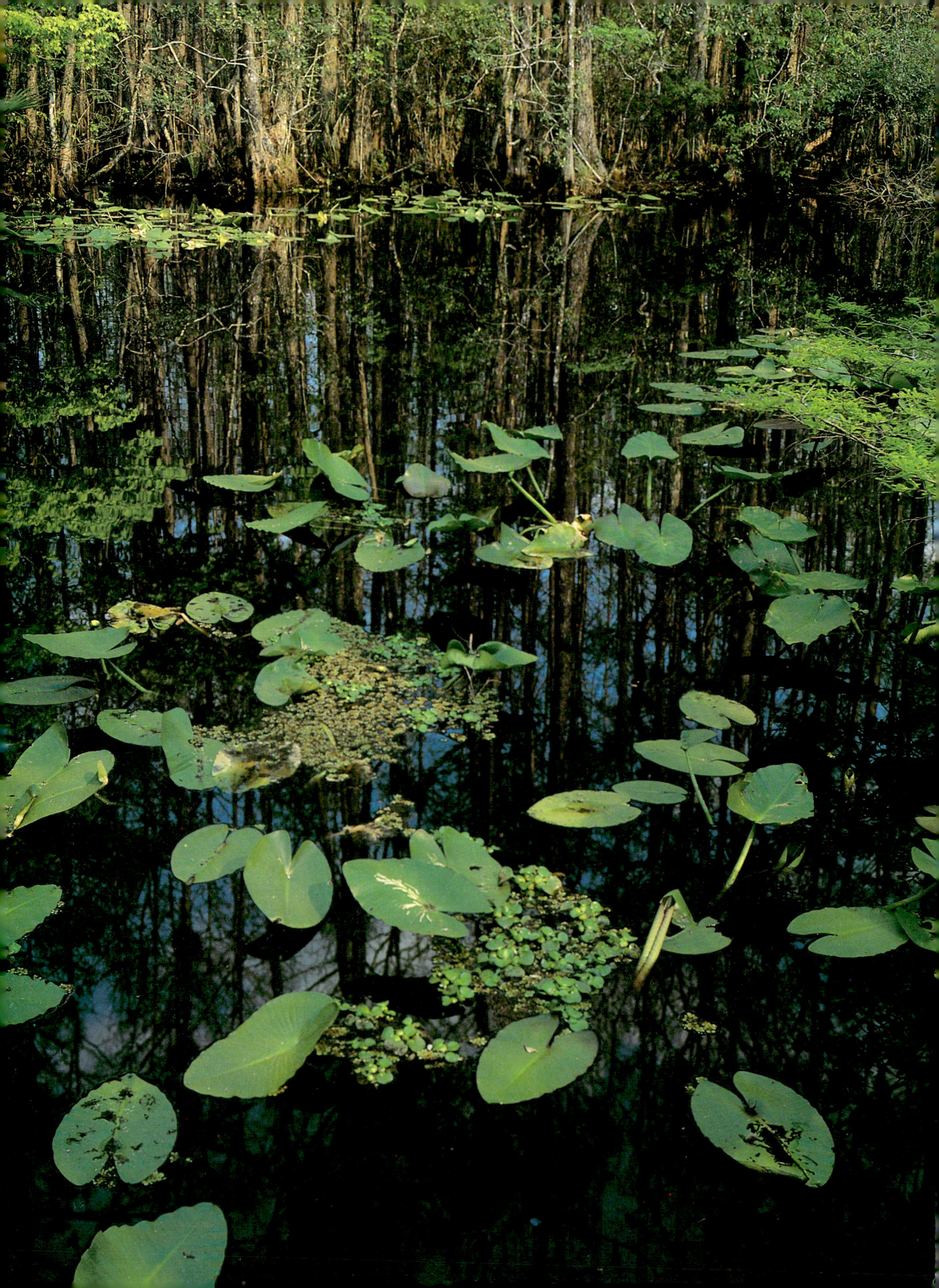

Miami Beach, Florida

Lily pads, Highlands Hammock State Park

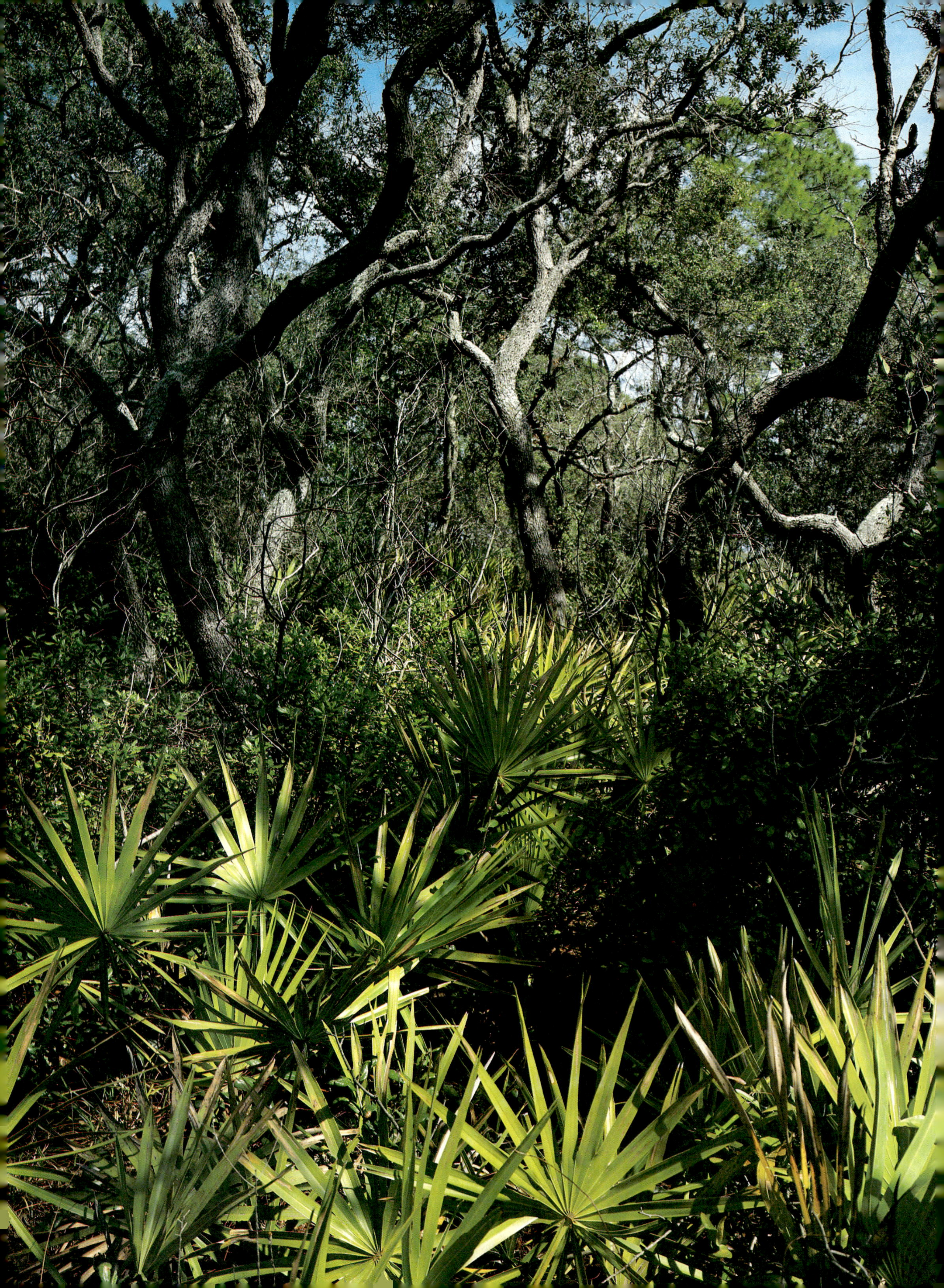

Another bequest of Florida's most celebrated entrepreneur is the Flagler Memorial Church, an imposing edifice built in memory of his daughter. The structure has an exterior of yellow brick and terra cotta and is topped by a soaring copper dome. Elegant, elongated stained-glass windows transform the sunlight into a blend of soft colors as it filters through them into the mellow interior of this Greco-Roman style chuch.

So St. Augustine is a town that shows its age and is proud of it. Not just because of the old buildings and monuments, but because it has been through so much in its sometimes turbulent history. The Spanish bombarded it, the British set fire to it and blockaded it, the Indians made things a little unquiet when they were being evicted, and in our time civil rights demonstrators brought some heat of their own to bear on the town. St. Augustine still has its problems, but remains a very pleasant place to be. It never made it as a winter resort on the scale envisioned by Henry Flagler, but it may, one day. The mild weather and spectacular peninsular setting make it a potent combination. And the beaches are just across the Matanzas River on the adjoining island of St. Augustine Beach.

Moving on down the coast, the auto traveller takes Highway A1A for the best look at the sea and the scenery. Except for brief interruptions, the road lies along the narrow sand spits that cap the mainland for most of the way and are separated from it by the Intracoastal Waterway. The Waterway is a favorite route for yachts and other pleasure craft on their way to the south coast and the Florida Keys. Either mode of travel can be pleasant; neither waterway nor road is crowded, except in the Miami area.

After a few towns and commercial attractions, scattered thinly along the way (Marineland of Florida is nearby), the next sizeable communities are Ormond Beach-Daytona Beach, dedicated, heart and soul, to tourism. Flagler and his railroad helped things get started, and then the automobile took over. Daytona is, of course, the mecca of fast-car afficionados, but a variety of efforts are made to attract and entertain people, whatever their tastes. Daytona's famous long (23 miles), wide (as much as 500 feet) beach is still there and cars may still be driven upon it—at 10 miles an hour.

Sixty miles south is Cape Kennedy, the space-age sand spit. Before the Kennedy Space Center moved in, the cape and nearby towns like Titusville, Cocoa, and Melbourne were quiet parts of the Florida east coast. With the buildup of the space age program, the area became a tourist draw. It still is, even though launchings are less frequent nowadays. On launching days, the rockets' white glare is reflected on the faces of thousands of watchers gathered at various good viewpoints, like Cocoa Beach, to gaze at the brilliant and thunderous birth of a space probe.

(Following pages) Sunrise, Miami Harbor

St. Marks National Wildlife Refuge

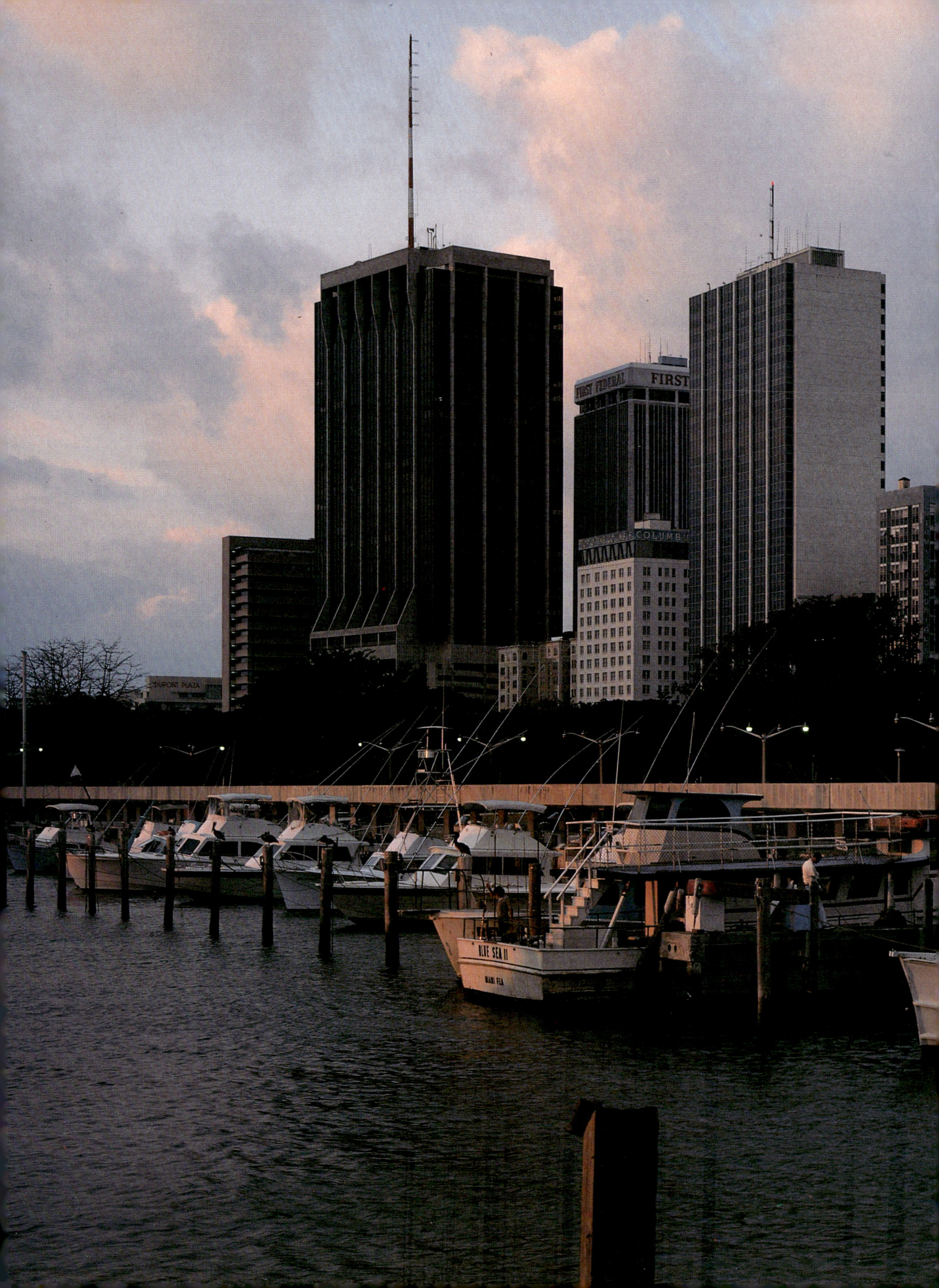
FIRST FEDERAL
FIRST
DUPONT PLAZA
BLUE SEA II

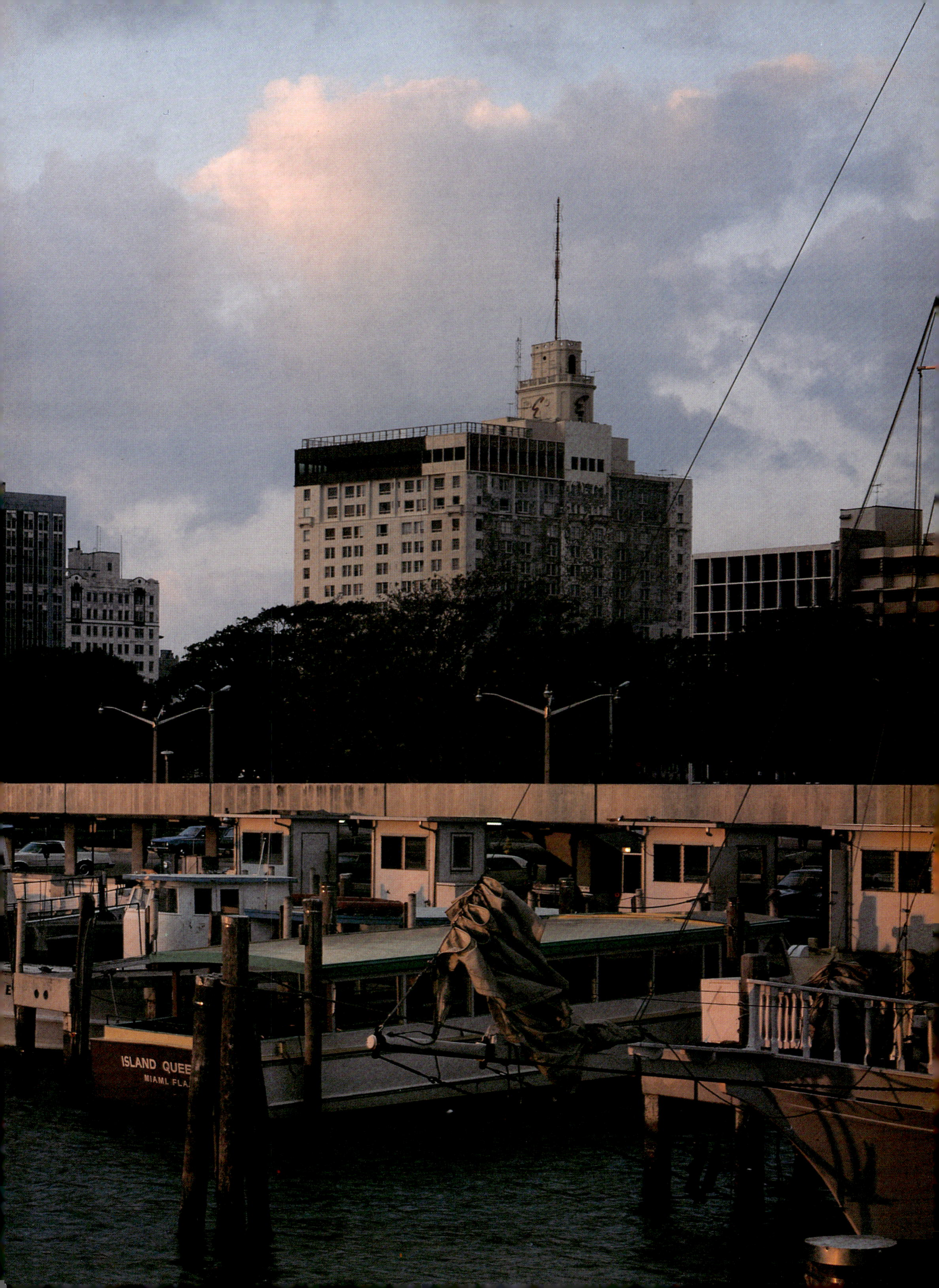
ISLAND QUEE
MIAMI FLA.

Some of the world's most publicized coastline begins to appear after Melbourne, which is about halfway along Florida's eastern shoreline. As one gets closer to West Palm Beach, the remnants of fishing villages give way to oceanfront construction catering to tourist multitudes, or to sleek new-look communities. But there are also some open, fairly wild spaces. Down around Vero Beach and Fort Pierce is the coastal citrus country, where some of the best oranges and grapefruit are grown. It's fertile land, the rich, black muck that surrounds Lake Okeechobee, and the second largest body of fresh water within the United States. This is winter vegetable country, and cane sugar country too.

Many kinds of fishing are available along this coast. There is bay fishing, ocean fishing, and just plain fishing from bridge walkways and piers. Below Fort Pierce is Hutchinson Island, a narrow sand spit with protected beaches where the loggerhead turtle comes ashore to lay its eggs. A hatchery on the island watches over the eggs, trying to even the odds a little in the turtles' favor.

Palm Beach and West Palm Beach each begin the parade of resort towns that seem to merge south to Miami in one long megalopolis. It is all very interesting, exciting, and beautiful. The great palms and the instant gardens proclaim that this is south Florida; added to these are the many non-native tropical plants with their lush foliage and incandescent blooms, blended with native species in the lavish abandon that so characterizes the Gold Coast. It may not be nature in the purest sense, but the sheer creativity of some of the displays make of them an art form.

To round the tip of Florida takes a boat, a plane, or a very watertight car. The two cross-peninsular highways through the Glades avoid the extreme southern perimeter. One of those roads—the Tamiami Trail—comes in on the west side close to Everglades City on the coast and Chokoloskee, a small island village just off shore. These two points are closely associated with the Ten Thousand Islands off the Gulf coast, a wild and complicated estuarine environment that can only be negotiated by boat. Until recently the skills of an experienced guide were required to find one's way through the maze of mangrove islands, tidal rivers, and bays. In 1968, the National Park Service marked out the Wilderness Waterway, a 99-mile route from Everglades City to Flamingo. A National Park service area and marina lies at the end of the road into Everglades National Park.

Before the Tamiami Trail gets to Naples on the Gulf side, it passes Collier-Seminole State Park, a sort of microcosm of the Everglades. The second part of the park's name acknowledges the fact that this is still very much Seminole country. A 4,760-acre wilderness preserve in the park's mangrove swamp represents the Everglades in its purest state, before western man ever penetrated it. The preserve,

Lagoon, Singing Tower and Mountain Lake Sanctuary

Cypress Swamp, Highlands Hammock State Park

Palms, Myakka State Park

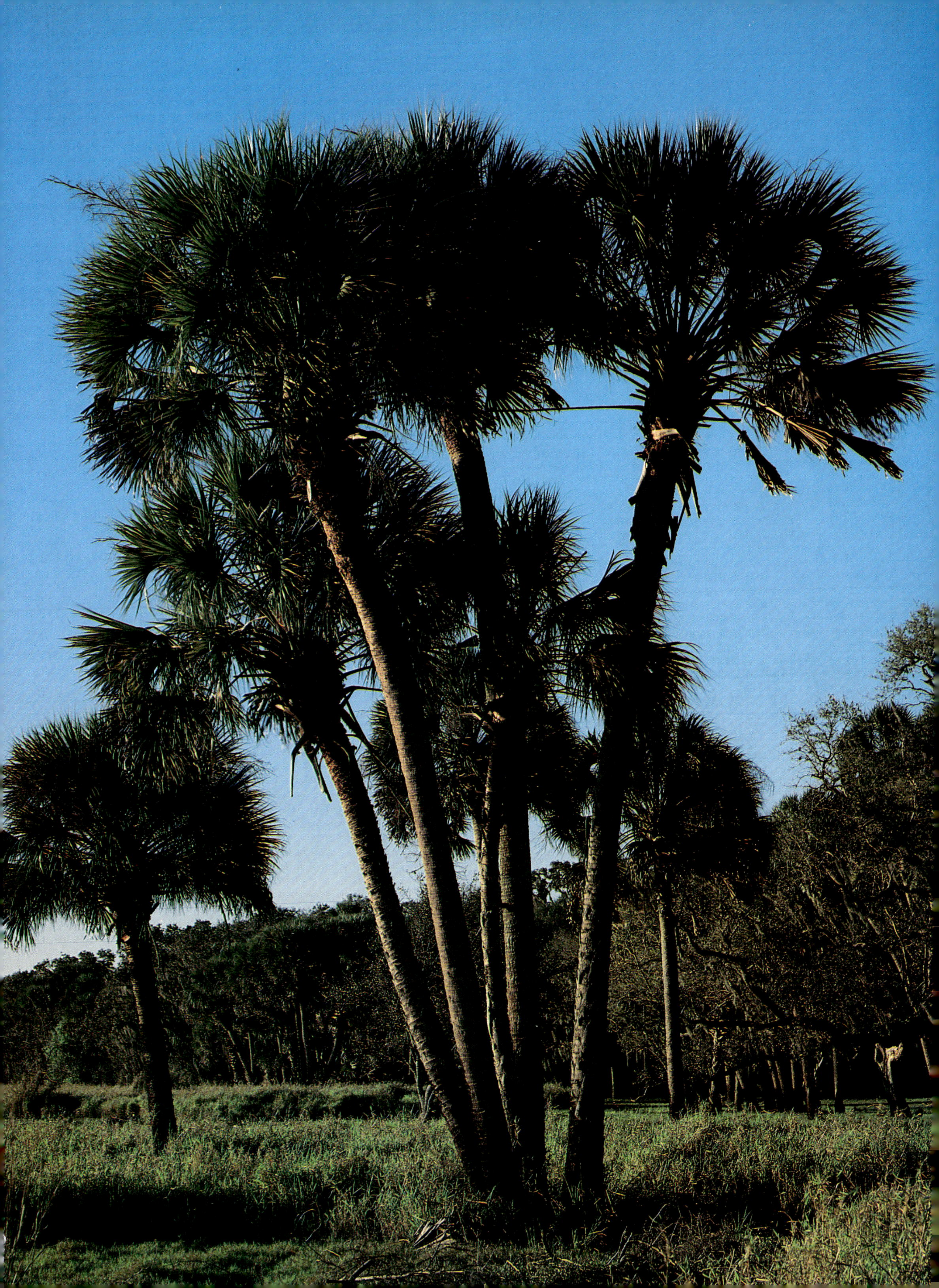

accessible by canoe, is a sanctuary for some endangered species, among which is the manatee. Tropical and subtropical trees, like the now rare royal palm, grow in the hardwood hummocks of the park. The diversity of the Everglades is further illustrated by the cypress swamps, salt marshes, and pine flatwoods.

Naples is a pleasant introduction to the southern Gulf coast. It is definitely a low-key community, with a different pace than the towns across the peninsula. Naples' long, unspoiled, white-sand beach is a rich treasure-house of shells, especially the spectacular big ones like conchs, whelks, tritons, moons, and pens. There are a great variety of other ones as well. Naples shares its reputation as a rich shell area with some other spots up and down the Gulf side. One of these is Marco Island a few miles south; the abundance of shells is only one aspect of the wealth of sea life that inhabits the shallow waters around the island.

Another place where shell-fanciers head for a rich harvest is Sanibel Island, just offshore from Fort Myers, 37 miles to the north. A recently built causeway now connects Sanibel and its twin island, Captiva, to the mainland. For this reason the islands have lost some of their remoteness and given up a great many shells.

On Sanibel there is a small wildlife refuge, where a variety of Florida's bird and animal life may be seen via a five-mile unsurfaced road through the preserve. The flow of visitors into the "Ding" Darling National Wildlife Refuge causes little anxiety among the refuge residents. So the visitor, if he parks the car and does some walking, is usually observed as much as observing, sometimes at very short range. All around you are birds—herons, ibises, egrets, pelicans, hawks, and so on—perched in the trees or standing with fierce concentration in a pond searching for an underwater lunch. The alligators live here too, even along the side of the road where they come up out of the swamp to do a little time in the sun.

Fort Myers itself is a pleasant place on the wide Caloosahatchee River. It's inland from the coast a few miles. For that reason, perhaps, it seems to be rather off-hand about being a south Florida resort community.

North from Fort Myers, US 41 swings past Punta Gorda and Port Charlotte over to the coast again. The pace quickens and the traffic thickens; the Florida Gulf central triumvirate are not far away: Sarasota—St. Petersburg—Tampa. There are some wonderful things in those places, including gorgeous beaches, idyllic (sometimes) islands, and beautiful bays. The combination of consistently fine weather, spectacular land-sea environments, and interesting and attractive cities with long strings of "outrigger" beaches has produced a tourist economy, catering to visitors whose homes are not likewise blessed by nature and climate.

Lilies, Torreya State Park

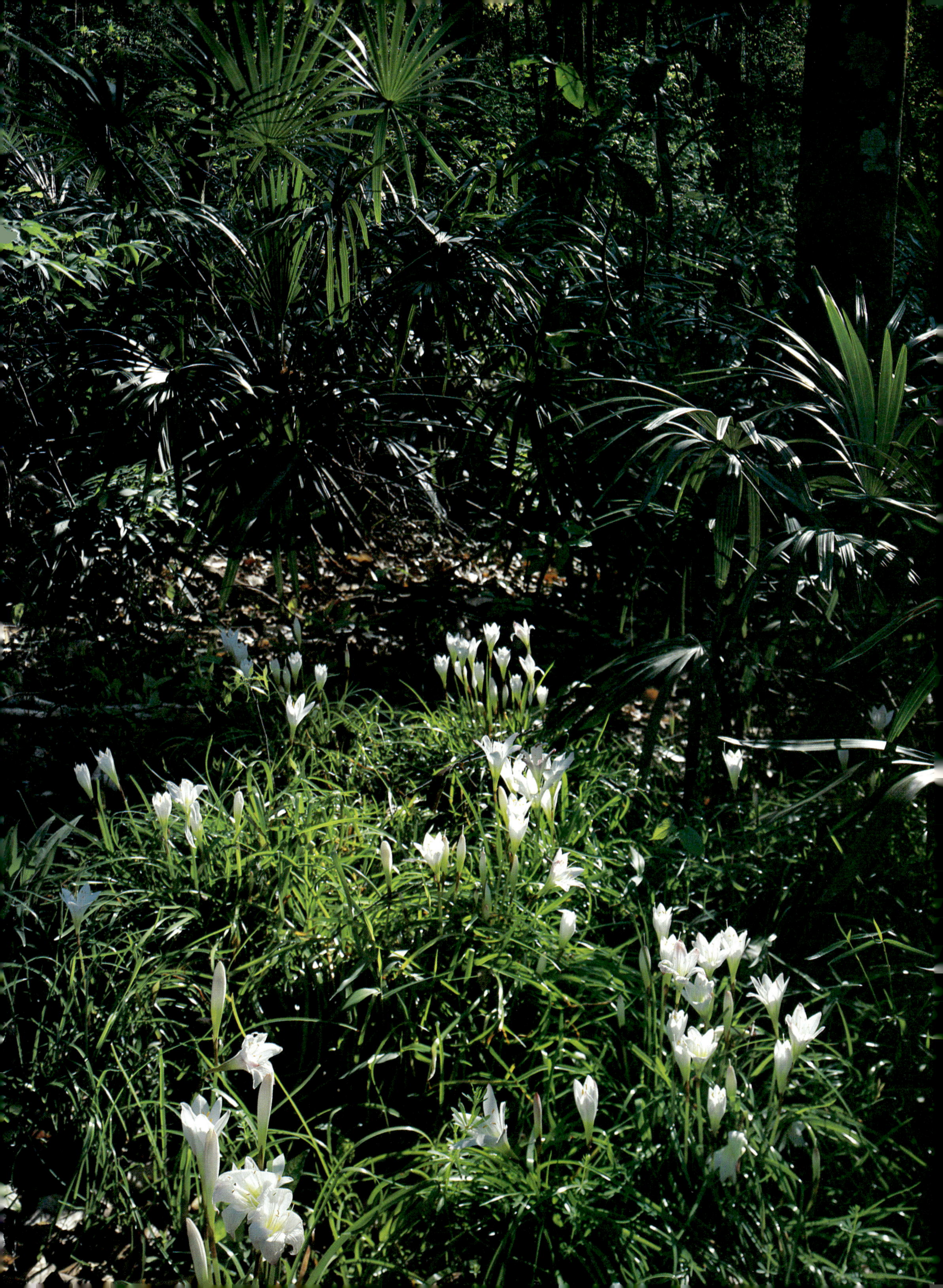

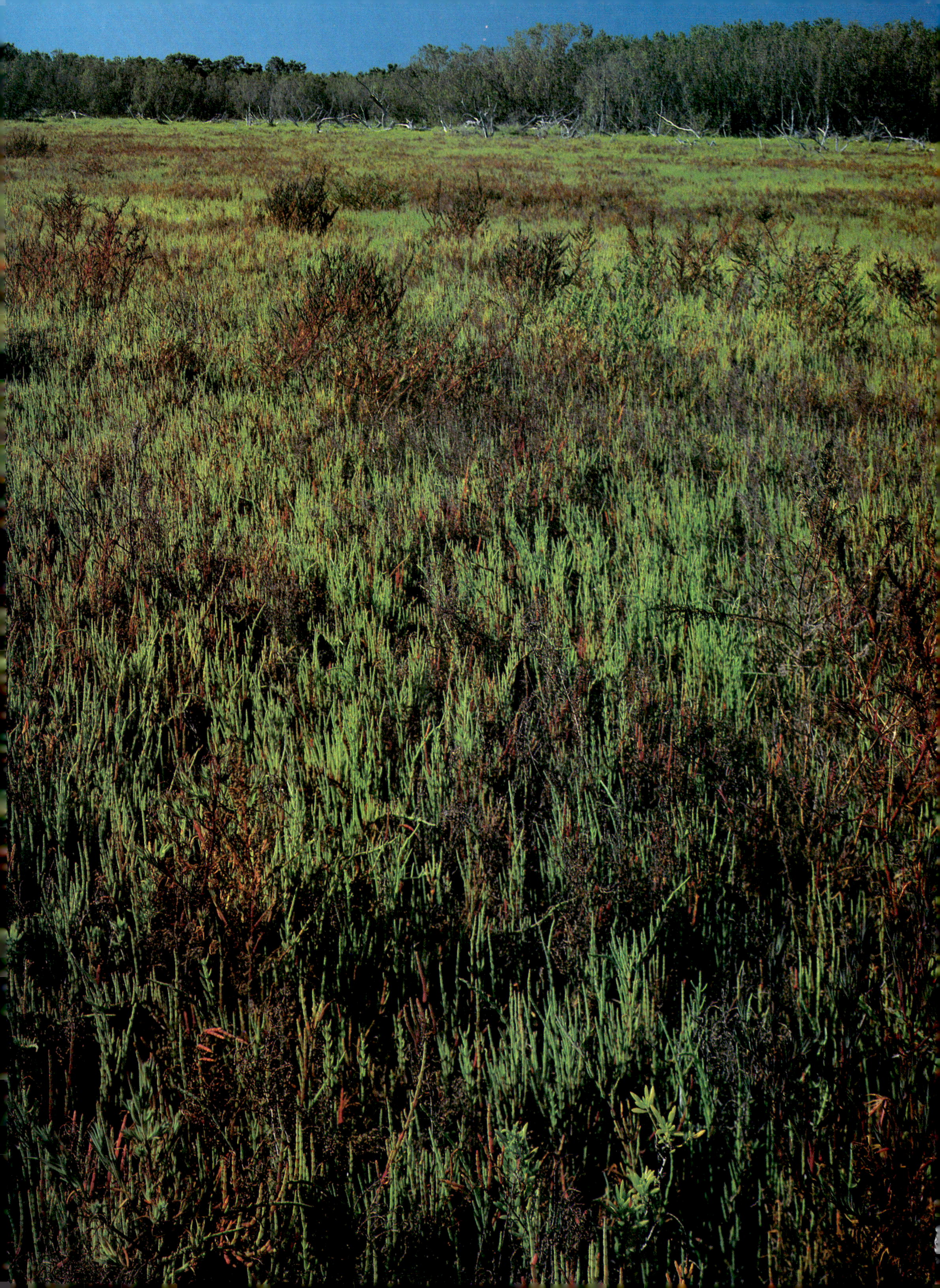

Celery Plant, Everglades National Park

Disney World

77

Photo Credits

ED COOPER—*page 8; page 18; page 27; page 43; page 49; page 80.*

BOB CLEMENZ—*pages 20-21; pages 28-29; pages 36-37; pages 52-53.*

JOHN GRONERT—*page 30; page 34; page 38; page 40; pages 44-45; page 46; page 62; page 65; pages 68-69; page 77.*

JOHN M. HALL—*page 11.*

JERRY SIEVE—*page 6; pages 12-13; page 14; page 17; page 23; page 24; page 33; page 35; page 39; page 42; page 47; page 50; page 55; page 56; page 58; page 59; page 61; page 63; page 64; page 66; page 71; page 72; page 73; page 75; page 76; page 78.*

Beautiful America Publishing Company

The nation's foremost publisher of quality color photography

Current Books

Alaska, Arizona, British Columbia, California, California Vol. II, California Coast, California Desert, California Missions, Colorado, Florida, Georgia, Hawaii, Los Angeles, Idaho, Illinois, Maryland, Michigan, Michigan Vol. II, Minnesota, Montana, Montana Vol. II, Mt. Hood (Oregon), New York, New Mexico, Northern California, Northern California Vol. II, North Idaho, Oregon, Oregon Vol. II, Oregon Coast, Oregon Mountains, Portland, Pennsylvania, San Diego, San Francisco, Texas, Utah, Virginia, Washington, Washington Vol. II, Washington D.C., Wisconsin, Yosemite National Park

Forthcoming Books

California Mountains, Indiana, Kentucky, Las Vegas, Massachusetts, Mississippi, Missouri, Nevada, New Jersey, North Carolina, Oklahoma, Ozarks, Rocky Mountains, San Juan Islands, Seattle, South Carolina, Tennessee, Vermont, Wyoming

Large Format, Hardbound Books

Beautiful America, Beauty of California, Glory of Nature's Form, Lewis & Clark Country, Western Impressions

(Following page) Sunset, Florida Keys

Washington Oaks Gardens State Park